The Dow Theory Today

THE DOW THEORY

TODAY

by

Richard Russell

publisher of Dow Theory Letters

RICHARD RUSSELL ASSOCIATES

NEW YORK, N.Y.

First published by

RICHARD RUSSELL ASSOCIATES
NEW YORK, N.Y.

Fraser Publishing Company Edition 1981
a division of
Fraser Management Associates, Inc.
Box 494
Burlington, Vermont 05402

Second Printing, 1985
Third Printing, 1989
Library of Congress Catalog Card Number: 81-68858
ISBN: 0-87034-061-1

PRINTED IN THE UNITED STATES OF AMERICA
DESIGNED BY *philip d. cole*

Introduction

This book consists of a collection of twelve articles which were written and published during the period of December, 1958, through December, 1960. The period was a particularly difficult one for investors and traders; for the market analyst (who must put his opinions on record) it was an even more trying period. Articles two through five in this book pertain to general Dow Theory or to market history as interpreted under Dow's Theory. Articles one and six through twelve deal with the price movements on the dates specified.

Most of what I have learned about markets has been gleaned from the writings of three men, Charles H. Dow, William P. Hamilton and Robert Rhea. If this book helps to perpetuate their sound ideas and principles it will have been worth the writing.

RICHARD RUSSELL
January 12, 1961
New York, N.Y.

Table of Contents

The Dow Theory Today

I

Dow Theory
Revisited

December 1, 1958

Periodically, after crucial and unexpected turns in the market, the study of the Dow Theory gains renewed attention from the public. Because a handful of Dow Theorists correctly interpreted last year's reaction and also predicted this year's historic advance, a good deal of interest has been revived today in this oldest and most dependable method of forecasting price movements and economic trends.

Now just what is the Dow Theory? Basically, it is a system based on the premise that the closing prices of the Dow-Jones Industrial and Rail Averages give us a complete index of all the knowledge, hopes and fears of everybody who knows anything about financial matters. Each investor, acting on what he knows of his own business and the economy, is represented in an emotionless bal-

3

ance which we call the Averages. For this reason, the effects of coming events (excluding acts of God) always are anticipated by the movements of these two indicators.

Talleyrand, the famous French foreign minister, once remarked: "I know somebody that knows more than anybody, and that is everybody." Financially speaking, that "everybody" is the market. When the majority of informed opinion feels that factors favorable to business are in the offing, stocks are purchased and the market advances. Conversely, when informed opinion feels that conditions are deteriorating, cash is preferred to equity and stocks are sold, thus touching off a decline.

※ ※

The Theory is over 60 years old. In 1897, Charles H. Dow, founder of the Dow-Jones News Service and *The Wall Street Journal*, devised the Dow-Jones Industrial and Rail Averages. Dow was the first editor of *The Wall Street Journal*, and besides having access to large amounts of financial information, he possessed a keen and analytical mind. He noticed that stocks did not drift aimlessly, but seemed to rise and fall in definite patterns. To prove his thesis, he formulated the now-famous Averages, and by plotting them back for a number of years, came upon the graphic proof for which he had been searching.

He concluded that there were three simultaneous movements in the market. The first was the great primary trend or tide. In a bull market, for example, this is a broad upward movement, interrupted by frequent reactions. The primary trend may last from one year to a great many years. The next movements are the so-called secondary reactions, which reverse and correct the tidal moves. They usually last from three weeks to three months, and tend to retrace one-third to two-thirds of the previous uncorrected primary moves. The final movements are the daily moves. These minor fluctuations admittedly can be manipulated by the news of the day. Although the least important, they are the ones to which the public pays most attention. The single movement which every investor must be aware of at all times is the primary trend. Investors always should invest with this primary tide.

Not to be confused with the foregoing three movements are the three phases of a bull market. These phases Dow and his successor as editor of *The Wall Street Journal*, the brilliant William P. Hamilton, recognized and charted in detail. Phase one is the rebound from the depressed conditions of the previous bear market. Here stocks return to known values. In the second and longest phase, shares advance in recognition of improving business and a rising economy. During the third phase they spurt skyward on the hopes and expectations of a continuing rosy future. This is the traditional period of great prosperity and unbounded optimism. It is here that the public enters the market wholeheartedly for the first time. The low-priced "cats-and-dogs" historically make great moves in this third phase, and market volume becomes excessive.

Under Dow Theory, it is a bullish sign when successive rallies penetrate previous high points, and ensuing declines terminate above preceding lows. It is a bearish indication when rallies fail to penetrate earlier highs, and ensuing declines carry below their former lows. It is crucial to remember that the movements of both Rail and Industrial Averages always must be considered together. The action of one Average must be confirmed by the other before reliable inferences can be considered. A penetration of one Average unconfirmed by the other is meaningless for prediction purposes and frequently can be deceptive.

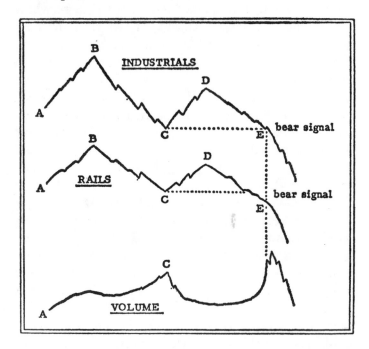

A change in the primary trend, indicating a reversal from bull to bear market, occurs on the following formation. First, a secondary reaction (see chart, B-C) takes place, lasting three weeks to three months and retracing about one-third to two-thirds of the preceding primary advance (A-B). It is what happens after this secondary reaction that is vitally important. Following the final low point of the reaction (C), there will be an advance of a few weeks or so (C-D), correcting the reaction (B-C).

If in due time the two Averages top their previous high point (B), the bull market will be taken as continuing. However, if one or both Averages refuse to go over the previous high point (B), and the two Averages then decline (on increasing volume), breaking the low point of the secondary reaction (C and E), we then must say that the bull market has ended and a bear market has been operating since the high point (B). After the bear market signal has been given, we then will go back and reclassify the entire secondary reaction (B-C) as the first primary swing in a new bear market, and the retracement (C-D) will be reclassified as the first secondary reaction (upward) in a bear market.

❦ ❦

Bear market signals, however, must not be oversimplified. The great Dow Theorist Robert Rhea wrote in 1938: "Beginners frequently make the mistake of basing conclusions wholly on the matter of penetration. Familiarity with the co-related factors such as duration, extent, activity, divergence, and secondary implications of primary bull markets is needed to make a correct diagnosis." Anyone who has studied the works of Hamilton and Rhea knows that it is only in the third and last phase of an extended bull market that a bear signal is valid. Ignorance of this fact has led to one of the most disastrous mis-readings of the Averages in modern stock market history.

Over and over again, the great Dow Theorists have warned us not to take a shallow, mechanical reading of the Averages while disregarding phases, duration and extent of the market movements. By calling a bear market on a "false" second-phase signal, the majority of the financial fraternity has committed one of the most costly errors in market annals.

Once the fact is accepted that bear market signals are valid only when they occur within the third phase of a bull market, the utmost importance must be attached to identifying the third phase. "This is the time," wrote Rhea, "when brokers and soothsayers prosper, and when an excited public, lured by the bait of advancing prices, buys stocks without regard to values, basing their action on nothing more than hopes and expectations." He observes that "this is the phase where worthless stocks are bought for no other reason than because they look cheap, and because gamblers hope they will double in price. This condition always has prevailed in the third phase of bull markets . . ."

※ ※

Again, said Rhea, "the final stage is sometimes recognizable because people then buy stocks simply because they go up, and because other people are buying them. They consider it old-fashioned to regard earnings or prospects. Speculation is rampant. In-and-out traders exchange their patched pants for gaudy attire, and become boardroom oracles. We soothsayers get to explaining why there never will be another bear market. Statisticians look backwards and figure out how it happened."

All this theory brings us to the big questions: where are we now, what phase are we in, and where are we going? In June, 1949, the greatest bull market in history was born. Few people suspected in this period of caution and fear that the Industrials, beginning at 161.60 on the Dow-Jones, in four years (1949–53) would climb to 293.79. At that point, a secondary reaction ended the first phase and took the Industrials back to 255.49. From there, the beginning of the second phase can be measured. The second phase is traditionally the longest one in a bull market, and it is in this phase that we may expect the most severe and deceptive reactions. From 255.49 in 1953 the Averages traveled to 521.05 in 1956, the greatest advance in stock market history. Rails also doubled, from 90.56 in 1953 to 181.23 in 1956. What followed makes for one of the great financial debates of history and one which is going on to this day.

In July, 1957, both Averages turned down, forecasting the sharpest business slump of the postwar period. From a high of 520.77 in July, the Industrials dropped some 20% to a low of 419.79 in October. In the same period, the rails dipped from 157.67 to 95.67. During that sharp three-month decline, expectations of a new bear market grew more widespread. However, from those depressed levels the market turned around once again, and began a spectacular new climb. The move carried the Rails to a recovery high of 157.91, and the Industrials to an all-time peak of 566.24 just ten days ago.

If it is true that a bear signal was given in 1957 when both Averages penetrated their previous lows, we must ask whether the market then was experiencing the symptoms of a typical third phase. Here a historical comparison is revealing. In 1946, at the height of the 1942–46 bull market, when the Dow-Jones Industrials hit 212.50, *Barron's* Low-Priced Stock Index was 173. The 1942–46 market admittedly was not a great bull market, compared to the present one. Yet during the entire period since 1946, *Barron's* Low-Priced Stock Index (after collapsing in the bear market that followed 1946) never returned to the highs of that year!

❦ ❦

During the entire 1956–57 period, this index hovered around 110–60. Does this seem like "rampant speculation?" Were the "cats-and-dogs" making their traditional third-phase moves? In 1956 and 1957, volume was running from one to three million shares daily. Does this appear to be "excessive volume"? In 1928 and 1929 (the only bull market which compares in duration and extent to this one) volume would clip along at a daily rate of four to six million shares for weeks at a time, many days showing well over six million.

Then how about the psychological atmosphere of 1956–57? Was it the type of atmosphere we would expect at the pinnacle of a great bull market? There were no less than six "scare" reactions during those two years. The crowd repeatedly was "shaken-out" of the market by the nerve-wracking news stories of the day. Hardly the type of "excitement" we expect in a third phase, where the financial skies traditionally are rosy. And most telling of all, the great 1957 "penetration" of the Averages through their previous lows took place amid the most depressing international news, topped off by a tight-money policy and the "Sputnik scare." No bear signal in stock market history has been given under similar conditions.

Traditionally, they come at a time when the crowd is rampantly bullish and hardly ready to "believe" the ominous signal. For instance, ten days after the 1937 bear signal was given, Robert Rhea wrote the following: "Except during 1929, there probably never was a time when soothsayers generally were as bullish as now."

During the next six months, a disastrous bear market wiped out about 50% of total stock values!

Dow Theorists know that upward moves in a bull market are long and plodding compared to the fast, often violent downward moves which occur during reactions. In a bear market, the exact opposite is true. Yet the reaction of 1957 wiped out 100 points in the Dow-Jones Industrials in just three months. It was an extremely rapid move, compared to the slow climb which preceded it—hardly bear-market action. And the return from the October lows took more than four times as long, or 14 months—a comparison which has extremely bullish implications. In other words, it took 14 months to retrace what three months had wiped out. The climb from the lows of October, 1957, was of the most typical bull market variety.

At the bottom of a bear market there is usually a period of prolonged dullness accompanied by very low volume. Yet the 1957 reaction ended on a burst of volume typical of a bull market secondary reaction. And since the October, 1957, lows, the trend of volume has been to recede on declines. In a bear market, on the contrary, volume expands when prices dip. Never, in fact, has there been a more obvious bullish formation than the picture the Averages have presented since the October lows.

❦ ❦

Now how about the extent of the decline in the "bear market"? We know that in a secondary reaction the Averages tend to retrace from one-third to two-thirds of the previous primary move. The Industrials began their second-phase advance from the 255.49 level in 1953. They then climbed an amazing 265 points, to 521.05. The 1957 secondary reaction wiped out 100 points, or about 38% of the previous second phase advance, a perfectly normal correction. Rails commenced their second-phase advance at 90.56 in 1953 and climbed 91 points to 181.23 in 1956. While the secondary reaction wiped out almost the entire advance, there are numerous precedents for this drastic decline in the history of the Averages. All in all, the reaction of 1957 was normal in both duration and extent.

It is this writer's opinion that we have been in the third phase of this bull market since the D-J Industrials registered the October, 1957, lows of 419.79. Considering that volume now is running on average above anything seen so far in this bull market, considering the new all-time highs recently recorded by the Industrials, considering the "in-gear" climb of the Rail Average, and considering the great moves now taking place in low-priced stocks, the indicators of a third phase now are present for the first time since this bull market began in 1949.

It is of interest, too, that Barron's Low-Priced Stock Index recently has passed its 1946 high for the first time in 12 years. This indicates that we may be seeing the beginning of crowd participation and rampant speculation in a coming great third-phase boom. The extent and duration of this move is a matter of individual opinion, and many Dow Theorists, including the writer, have their own notions as to how far and how long the present third phase will last. Since this is not a matter of interpretation, but at best an educated guess, this article will not attempt to go into the extent and duration of the third phase.   ૧૨ ૧૨

All in all, then, the Dow Theory, while not infallible, still is considered by many the most reliable barometer available for predicting the trend of stocks and the economy. Mechanically, the Dow Theory is a simple charting of the Averages, to recognize bullish or bearish signals. The art of the Dow Theory consists of interpreting the movements of the two Averages, after taking into consideration volume, extent and duration of movements, confirmation, timing, and phases. The study of the Dow Theory, like so many other studies, entails the danger that a little knowledge may be worth less than none at all.

II

What Dow
Wrought

February 16, 1959

A navigator, ignorant of the use of charts and unfamiliar with the ocean's currents, would need more than ordinary luck to bring his ship to port. Experienced seamen might well accuse him of gambling with the lives of all aboard. There are many who believe that a trader who enters the stock market without a knowledge of the implications of the price-movements is gambling with his capital in much the same way. Often, he is gambling with the capital of others.

Few amateur speculators are fortunate enough to be immediately successful in the stock market. The author's first transactions were probably less successful than most. After many years of operating on the basis of every technique and system that I could classify as in any way acceptable, I decided either to make sense of the market

14

or take my permanent leave. Through luck, or perhaps through the process of elimination, I came upon the Dow Theory. In attempting to disprove this method as well, I became a convert. It is probable that many Dow Theorists are made in this same way.

The name Dow Theory is a household word wherever securities are mentioned. Yet I can think of no body of financial knowledge about which so little is known, either to the investing public or the Wall Street fraternity. The few books which explain the Theory are now out of print; there are no national publications which attempt to teach the Theory; its great practitioners are for the most part either deceased or silent. Where are the real Dow Theorists, then? The answer is that they are busy managing successful businesses, directing the policy of banks or institutions, or practicing their professions of medicine, law, and accounting. They know that the rewards for the study and correct use of the Theory have been so great, and the penalties for ignoring it so severe, that few of them would care to disregard its implications.

This first article of a series will consist of a general description of the Dow Theory. Its principles are not difficult to understand, they are, however, more difficult to accept. In these articles I have made use of many direct quotes, perhaps an excessive amount. But the Theory as it stands today is not mine; it is the work of Dow, Hamilton, and Rhea. Where practical, I have presented their ideas in their own words.

The basic tenets of the Dow Theory were conceived by Charles H. Dow, founder of Dow, Jones & Co., and first editor of *The Wall Street Journal*. Hamilton, his understudy at *The Journal*, describes him as ". . . almost judicially cold in the consideration of any subject. His perfect integrity and good sense commanded the confidence and respect of every man on Wall Street, at a time when there were few efficient newspaper men covering the financial section, and still fewer with any knowledge of finance." Dow had been a floor trader on the Stock Exchange for a number of years and possessed an exceptional financial background for a newspaper man. "Dow was almost too cautious to come out with a flat, dogmatic statement of his Theory . . ." observes Hamilton, "It must be disinterred from those editorials, where it is illustrative and incidental and never the main topic of discussion." The way to the Dow Theory, it seems, was not easy even for Dow's protege.

Dow, Jones & Co. had published a single combined Average of stocks up to the year 1897. It was Dow who conceived of the two separate averages, rails and industrials. This division had far-reaching consequences as we shall see later. It is incredible that Dow drew most of his conclusions about the movements of stocks with only five years of the recorded averages with which to work. He died in 1902, the greatest part of his writing having appeared in the years 1901–2. All that Dow ever wrote was published by *The Wall Street Journal*. It is unfortunate that he was not a more prolific writer.

The phrase, Dow's Theory, was never used by Dow himself. It was coined by his friend and admirer, S. A. Nelson. Dow's complete editorials were assembled by Nelson in a little book entitled the "A.B.C. of Stock Speculation," which was published in 1902. A careful reading of this book will convince one that Dow did not envision his Theory as a device for predicting the trend of the market. He used his averages more as a gauge of the current state of stocks and the economy. It was Dow who discovered the heretofore unsuspected fact that "The market is not like a balloon, plunging hither and thither in the wind. As a whole it represents a serious, well-considered effort on the part of farsighted and well-informed men to adjust prices to such values as exist or which are expected to exist in the not-too-remote future." In other words, Dow discovered that stocks move in definite trends and for definite reasons.

As a student of market psychology, Dow had few peers. His observations concerning the emotions of the crowd and the movements of stocks form an intricate part of the Theory. "There is always a disposition in people's minds to think the existing conditions will be permanent. When the market is down and dull, it is hard to make people believe that this is the prelude to a period of activity and advance. When prices are up and the country is prosperous, it is always said that while preceding booms have not lasted, there are circumstances connected with this one which make it unlike its predecessors and give assurance of permanency. The one fact pertaining to all conditions is that they will change." This statement, written fifty-six years ago by Dow, has been borne out by history ever since. In all, he left us a body of principles out of which an entirely new concept of the market was built. To him, every technical study of stocks from the Dow Theory to the charting of individual stocks owes its beginning. He was the pioneer in a new way of market thinking. Many of his ideas will be discussed in this article, others will be dealt with in future articles.

William P. Hamilton, Dow's understudy at *The Journal*, and later its editor for twenty-five years, developed the Theory and first adapted it as a method for predicting the trend of stocks and the economy. Hamilton, in an historic series of editorials published in *Barron's* and *The Wall Street Journal*, consistently and successfully forecasted the trend of the market. Any student who will give Hamilton's work even a cursory examination will concede that the movements of the averages, when properly interpreted, do provide us a barometer with which to predict coming events. Hamilton's articles received wide acclaim at the time, and much to his regret, they were used by many as tips on the trend of stocks. Hamilton never intended them as such, and in an effort to thwart the tipsters he spaced his editorials as far apart as possible.

His classic book, "The Stock Market Barometer," created a storm of controversy when it was published in 1922 and this storm lasted for many years thereafter. "What we need," wrote Hamilton, "are soulless barometers, price indexes and averages to tell us where we are going and what we may expect. The best, because the most impartial, the most remorseless of these barometers, is the recorded average of prices in the stock exchange." Later, he states, "It cannot too often be repeated that the stock market, while adjusting itself to the unexpected, as in the secondary reactions, is based not upon surrounding conditions but upon what may be expected as far ahead as the combined intelligence of the market can see." Most of Hamilton's work was directed to the purpose of proving the predictive value of the Dow Jones Averages when properly interpreted. Over and over again he stressed this point. "The market does not trade upon what everyone knows, but upon what those with the best information can foresee. There is an explanation for every stock market movement somewhere in the future, and the much talked of manipulation is a trifling factor." As a warning to businessmen he said, "There is no business so small that it can afford to disregard the stock market barometer. Certainly there is no business so large that it dare disregard it." Hamilton left us with a wealth of wisdom and theory, but it was a body of knowledge that required great effort and understanding to ferret out and systematize.

It remained for Robert Rhea to handle this monumental task. Rhea was, in this writer's opinion, the greatest of all readers of the averages. True, he had Dow's and Hamilton's observations to guide him as well as many more years of the charted averages to study. Confined to his bed because of a wartime plane crash, Rhea possessed the intuitiveness of an artist, the analytical power of a mathematician, and the writing ability of a superior novelist. His unremitting study of the movements of the averages, and his brilliant deductions concerning these movements rate him as the third of a great triumvirate. One cannot help sympathizing with Rhea as he writes, "Had it been possible to reduce the forecasting implications of the averages to a definite arithmetical formula, I probably would have found it, because nobody ever sought the rainbow's end more diligently than I."

Robert Rhea's definitive book on the Dow Theory first appeared in chapter form in *Barron's* in 1932. As an explanation of the Theory, it has never been equaled. He later wrote his "Story of the Averages," which is an excellent source of information for serious students of the price-movements. One can only guess at the extent of Rhea's labors as he comments on the difficulties of a fellow Dow Theorist: "Mr. Collins, like this writer, had to dig out the 'Theory' from Hamilton's writings. I have often thought of asking him how long it took him to become reasonably confident of his ability to read the averages."

"The business community has a tendency to go from one extreme to the other," observed Dow. To those who have studied the market and its movements these words have a ring of undeniable truth. Yet to the average investor and to many a professional, who together have watched their funds increase through a long bull market, the fact that the stock market is subject to bull and bear primary trends often comes as an unpleasant bit of hindsight. Many investors hold stocks straight through a major decline. They believe that since they own only "blue-chips" they are not speculators. The next bear market, however, will teach them the unpleasant lesson that they are not only speculators but foolish gamblers. The idea that there is a body of knowledge that claims to predict the trend of the economy will doubtless strike these people as little less than an insult. Yet in proof, this series asks of the reader nothing more than an unbiased hour or so. Hamilton once observed that "In the mind of the demagogue, Wall Street can never be forgiven for being right when he is wrong."

The tools of the Dow Theory consist of the daily closing prices of the Dow Jones industrial and rail averages and the daily volume of total transactions. For convenience, we prefer to enter these indicators on a graph or chart. There are also a few Dow Theory principles which must be understood and eventually accepted if one is to learn to use the implications of the averages as a guide to investing. These principles should be studied carefully, for they are the laws of the Theory. They are listed here in outline form, as a matter of convenience. Most will be covered more thoroughly later.

1. The basic premise of the Theory is that the averages discount everything. The closing prices of the Dow Jones rail and industrial averages give us a complete index of everything known by anybody that can possibly affect the economy and corporate profits (excluding acts of God). "Consciously or unconsciously, the movements of prices reflect not the past but the future. When coming events cast their shadows before, the shadows fall on the New York Stock Exchange." (Hamilton)

2. The market consists of three movements all of which may be operating simultaneously. The first is the great tide or primary trend, which is usually referred to as a bull or a bear market. It is a relentless and all-engulfing force and may last anywhere from a year to a great number of years. Wars, politics, tightening money, disasters, nothing stops the great tide until it reaches its ultimate destination. The next movements are the secondary reactions, and these serve to correct the primary tide. Secondaries temporarily reverse the tidal movement, usually retracing one-third to two-thirds of the previous uncorrected primary swing. The third movements are the minor or daily fluctuations. These are the least important of the three, but they are the ones which receive by far the most attention from the public.

3. A primary bull market is a broad upward movement of stocks interrupted by frequent secondary reactions. There are three phases in a bull market. The first is the return to known values following the depressed conditions of the previous bear market. The second and usually

the longest phase is caused by the response of stocks to bettering business conditions and improved corporate profits. The third phase is characterized by feverish speculation, rampant inflation, and a highly promising economic outlook. Here, as Rhea tells us, "stocks are advanced on hopes and expectations."

4. A primary bear market is a broad downward movement interrupted by frequent secondary reactions (upward). A bear market serves to correct the excesses of the previous bull market and does not end until the worst that may happen has been fully discounted in the price structure. There are three phases in a bear market. In the first phase stocks sell minus the "hopes and expectations" of the previous bull market. The second and longest phase represents a reflection of worsening business conditions and decreasing corporate profits. In the last phase stocks sell at distress or liquidation prices, regardless of their earnings or lines of value. "It is the third phase of a bear cycle when people sell their good stocks, held against a rainy day, because it is raining," observed Rhea.

5. The trend of the market is determined as follows: Successive rallies advancing above previous high points with ensuing declines terminating above preceding low points are taken as bullish indications. Rallies that fail to penetrate preceding high points with ensuing declines breaking preceding low points carry bearish indications.

6. In determining the trend, it is a never to be forgotten rule that the movements of both averages must be considered together. The movement of one average must always confirm the other (although not necessarily on the same day), and conclusions drawn from the action of one average unconfirmed by the other are usually de-

ceptive. The confirmation principle is based on logic. If there is to be a valid increase in manufacturing and production, there will also be an accompanying increase in shipping and transportation. Goods produced, if they are not to sit idly in the warehouses, must be distributed to their destinations. If distribution occurs, some of it will be by rail. Regardless of the fact that other forms of transportation are now competing with the rails, an increase in shipping must affect the rails to some favorable extent. It is not necessary for the rail average to move to new highs in each succeeding bull market, but within a given bull market rails must merely advance above preceding high points to confirm.

7. Volume tends to expand in the main direction of the trend. In a bull market, advances accompanied by increasing volume or declines on diminishing volume are taken to be bullish. Conversely, in a bear market, declines are accompanied by increasing volume and advances show diminishing volume. Volume should always be studied as a trend (relative to what has preceded) and conclusions drawn from a single day's volume are often misleading.

8. "Lines" are formations in which both averages remain within an area of about 5% for a period of two weeks or longer. A line indicates a period of very evenly matched buying and selling. A penetration of both averages above their line limits indicates that the buying (accumulation) was superior to the selling (distribution) and is a prediction of higher prices to come. Penetration of both averages through their lower line limits indicates that sellers were better informed than buyers and is a prediction of lower prices to follow. It is not necessary for both aver-

ages to break out of a line on the same day but a penetration of one average without the other will more often than not prove deceptive.

9. The word penetration, under Dow Theory, implies any movement through a given point of one cent or more. Although some schools demand one dollar or more as a valid penetration signal, there are a few cases in the past where this interpretation has proved a costly one.

10. The primary and secondary movements are not susceptible to manipulation. It is conceded possible for a group to alter the price of a single stock or even the minor (daily) movement of the market. Hamilton often repeated, however, that the Federal Reserve, together with the Bank of England, did not have enough money to manipulate the primary or the secondary trend.

After reading the foregoing, readers may ask, what makes a bull or a bear trend inevitable? Is this some mystic Dow Theory concept; if not, where is the explanation? "The pragmatic basis for the theory," explained Hamilton, "lies in human nature itself. Prosperity will drive men to excess, and repentance for the consequence of these excesses will produce a corresponding depression." In the depths of a depression the storekeeper will discover that he has become overly cautious; he has allowed his inventory to fall even below daily sales. He decides that prices are attractive and increases his stock above mere daily needs. The worker, now perhaps searching for a job instead of higher wages, becomes a saver, regardless of his reduced income. Thrift will be the order of the day, and the businessman, finding money cheap, will consider expanding. Dullness turns to activity, activity breeds optimism. Later, this gives way to speculation, then to inflation, spiraling wages and higher money rates. And again the entire structure, snapping under the strain of a myriad of economic ills, collapses, and the spectre of depression once more rides the air. Curiously enough, an impartial study of history reveals that the more government intervenes in an attempt to minimize the severity of cycles, the more extreme and violent they seem to become. For instance, the bear market which began in 1937 was one of the most drastic, considering its duration of only a year, that has occurred in modern history.

Few people are aware that Dow stressed values above everything else. "To know values," he stated, "is to comprehend the meaning of the movements of the market." The true investor, Dow believed, is the man who knows and buys values. Of them he writes, "The thought with great operators is not whether a price can be advanced, but whether the value of the property which they propose to buy will lead investors and speculators six months hence to take stock at figures from 10 to 20 points above present prices." Hamilton was a shrewd judge of values and he wrote in March, 1921, just as a bull market was commencing, "Cheap stocks are never attractive. This is no Chestertonian paradox but a matter of record. If cheap stocks were attractive there would be an active market today, with an interested and even excited public." In other words, Hamilton believed that stocks here were selling below their line of values.

But if a man is a judge of values and merely buys when stocks seem cheap, what need has he for the Dow Theory? In answer, I am sure Hamilton would have said, my own opinion may be excellent, but it is only the verdict of the averages that I will put my money on. It was the market that Hamilton trusted above all, and he quoted one of America's greatest financiers as saying, "If I had 50% of all the knowledge that is reflected in the movements of stocks, I am confident that I would be far better equipped than any other man on Wall Street."

The pattern of the averages reflects the trend of values, and it is tomorrow's appraisals that the Dow Theorist seeks. U.S. Steel common sold as high as $261 in late 1929. An intelligent investor might have felt justified in paying a price of $60 for Steel in 1931; it probably looked cheap here. But there was nothing in the averages that year to indicate an end to the bear market. In 1932, only one year later, Steel sold for $22. Dow Theorists have learned to buy when the market itself has given its "bloodless verdict." They do not trade on the opinions or hunches of any single man or group of men.

The Dow Theory is a completely technical approach to the market. It derives nothing from business statistics, indexes of production, economic reports, or any of the other thousands of facts that make up a study of the fundamental condition of the country. Operating on the principle that the averages take all these systems and much more into consideration, the Theory becomes a study of the movements of the averages themselves. The Dow Theorist believes that most of the fundamentalist's facts are already history. The market is not interested in yesterday or today, it is concerned only with tomorrow. It is in the nature of the averages to contain all of the fundamentalists' facts plus the judgments and opinions of thousands of insiders, speculators, investors and businessmen, each viewing the market from the standpoint of his own business and the general economy.

Hamilton illustrated this when he wrote, "The farmers say . . . 'what does Wall Street know about farming?'

Wall Street knows more than all the farmers put together ever knew, with all that the farmers have forgotten. It can, moreover, refresh its memory instantly at any moment. It employs the ablest of the farmers, and its experts are better even than those of our admirable and little appreciated Department of Agriculture, whose publications Wall Street reads even if the farmer neglects them." Against this knowledge contained in the averages, says the Dow Theorist, the fundamentalist can seldom, if ever, win.

Many investors do not understand that the market is constantly discounting news. They are not aware that in the majority of cases, the "inside" information which they have just come upon is already built into the price of a stock or the averages. They are confused when a bearish piece of news is released, they sell their holdings, and the market advances. "News known, is news discounted," said Hamilton, and in an amazing amount of cases, the market has already discounted information which the amateur is convinced is of the most secret variety.

It should be remembered that the averages care not a whit for the number of people who may be buying or selling. The crowd, as such, does not make the market. It is the side with the greatest amount of purchasing dollars or the side with the largest amount of stock to sell that makes the trend. The averages register the majority opinion of money, not people.

The Dow Theory is based on empirical evidence. Its laws have been tested through formations and phases, confirmations and penetrations since 1897. The Dow Theorist knows that when rails advance above a previous high and industrials confirm the rail move, a general market rise will follow. He knows that when a bear signal is given in the third phase of a bull market, the back of a bull market is broken, regardless of the fact that the economy of the country at the time will more than likely appear exceedingly bright. To the person who has not studied the history of the price-movements, this is a difficult bit of reasoning to swallow. For one is more often than not acting against his emotions when he follows the implications of the Theory. It is not easy to buy heavily when a bull signal is given near the bottom of a bear market and while the majority of economists are talking of even worse things to come.

But the Theory is not a "system" for beating the market. Only the amateur can hope to discover such a device. The experienced investor is satisfied with a theory which, through hard work and diligent study, will allow him to make perhaps seven out of ten correct decisions while cutting short his mistakes. Nor is the Theory to blame if a new student allows his wishes to dictate to his better judgment. If he sells at the end of a long decline just as the market is preparing for an advance, is it the Theory's fault? In all probability, he has not really studied it, but owning a set of charts of the industrials alone, he calls himself a Dow Trader. For the gambler or scalper, the Theory is a useless study. It will never teach him to beat the market. Rhea remarked that this greedy fraternity ". . . consist of those who try to capitalize the daily movements. They do not know that, in the long run, an amateur cannot beat a professional. They go against the game of a floor trader (who is a professional) and try to beat him. Should the amateur's skill at 'in-and-out' trading exceed the professional's, the former would still lose because the floor trader pays no commissions. This group seems to gamble in pool stocks and gulp down 'tips' with relish. A man who habitually follows 'tips' is hopeless, and neither Dow's Theory nor anything else can help him."

In this writer's opinion, the greatest reward that can come to the student of the Dow Theory is that it teaches him to think for himself. The man who has learned to read the averages and can intelligently and unemotionally form his own conclusions does not require the services of another. He can ignore the tipster, the perpetual bull or bear, and the wishes, hunches, and inside information of the boardroom habitue. More important, he will learn to master his own emotions and fears. I do not know of a single Dow Theorist who has not at one time or another admitted that most of his mistakes were made when he trusted the implications of the averages too little and his own opinions too much.

The next article will take up the primary trends, the secondary reactions, what they mean, and how we can identify them. We will also go into their implications to the investor and trader.

III

Bull or Bear
Market?

March 23, 1959

❋♪❋♪❋♪❋ Wall Street contains many minds and perhaps as many opinions. One thing on which most analysts agree, however, is the crucial importance of knowing the direction of the market's primary trend. Indeed, it is incredible that so few amateurs or professionals, at a given time, can present evidence to prove logically that a bull or a bear market is in progress. If a man is unable to ascertain the direction of the primary trend, it is reasonable to assume that he also may be unable to detect the conditions which signal a turn in that trend. Yet no other phenomenon has proved so costly to security holders as this reversal of the tide from bull to bear market.

"Wall Street is inherently bullish," observed William

P. Hamilton. "One reason for this is that the financial district does not make money in a bear market, contrary to the idea of those people who think that then is the time when the Street reaps its harvest, and wickedly turns disaster to its own advantage. Wall Street lives on commissions, and not on what it might make by selling short the securities that it originates."

❦ ❦

During an extended bull market, investors are prone to accept bullishness as a way of life. "What of the occasional reaction?" the amateur retorts. "Aren't the stocks that I purchased a year ago higher than ever now?" And so the groundwork is laid for ever-increasing confidence, bigger and bolder speculation, and more and more optimism. As Rhea noted in 1935: "Chronic bulls grow fat, and sheep's wool grows long. Ordinarily when such conditions prevail, stocks are nearing the date when the bloodless verdict of the market will appraise them ex-hopes and expectations."

Primary bear markets are born amid the prosperity of the third or boom phase of the preceding bull market. They result from, and serve to correct, periods of inflation, speculation, and economic excess. During a long, exciting advance, Hamilton would warn his readers that "no tree grows to the sky." This advice may seem absurdly obvious; yet it generally is scorned near the pinnacle of a bull market. All primary swings, whether bull or bear, tend to overrun themselves. Just as bull markets expire in periods of unrealistic optimism, bear markets exhaust themselves amid times of hopeless depression.

❦ ❦

This does not imply that all bull markets are 1929s or that all bear markets are 1932s. There is little or no relationship between one bull market and another, either in duration or extent. There is, however, a relationship between a bull market and the bear market which directly follows. History shows that the more inflationary and speculative the former, the more drastic the latter. In duration, bear markets average about 60% as long as bull markets. In extent, most bear markets retrace at least 50% of the preceding bull market. Of 14 bear markets since 1896, only two (1899–1900 and 1946–47) failed to wipe out at least half the gains of the preceding bull market.

Strangely enough, the only relationship between a bear market and the directly following bull market occurs in the latter's first phase. It seems that the more severe the final bear swing, the more powerful the rebound in the first phase of the new bull market, as stocks return to known values. From this point on, however, the new bull market is figuratively "on its own."

Physicists know that for every force there is an equal and opposing counter-force. Though this law cannot be applied exactly to the stock market, the history of the primary trend of prices from 1921 to today suggests many valid comparisons. In 1921, the Dow-Jones Industrials began to turn up, at 63.90. They advanced during the next eight years to the unheard-of level of 381.17. In many ways, the years 1928 and 1929 remain unequaled for sheer, speculative intensity. The unforeseen correction which followed 1929 carried the Average all the way down to 41.22 in July, 1932. Then a new impulse drove Industrials to 194.40 in 1937, after which another violent bear market returned them to 98.95 only one year later.

A series of inconclusive "baby" bull and bear markets followed.

The impulse for which the market was searching came in 1942. Amid World War II, and the confusion of a thousand imponderables, a new primary advance began. Dramatically enough, this new bull market got under way in April, well before it was apparent that the war had turned in favor of the Allies. Industrials climbed from 92.96 in 1942 to 212.50 in 1946. Here, as noted, a bear market refused to retrace 50% of the preceding bull market. It was almost as if the upward momentum had not been fully spent. An insignificant bull and bear cycle followed for the next few years.

❦ ❦

That brings us to 1949, a year in which the public was singularly uninterested in stocks; daily volume on the New York Stock Exchange was averaging less than one million shares. A severe recession was upon the country, and many felt that the long-promised postwar depression had arrived. Yet amid this caution and fear, with the Average at 161.60, history's greatest bull market was born. It had taken 20 years to produce this tremendous undercurrent; few were aware that it had arrived. But the primary trend would not be denied. Through three recessions, through war scares, through Korea, Suez, Lebanon, tight money, Eisenhower's heart attack, Sputnik, and the misinformed warnings of a thousand analysts, the Averages surged upward. Yet Dow Theorists know that this great bull market, too, having planted the seeds of its own destruction in speculation and inflationary excess, some day will strangle itself, as have all others before it.

During bull markets, the Dow Theorist usually adopts

one of two methods of operation. He may purchase his securities early, when the primary trend first shows signs of turning up, and hold them through the entire bull market, selling only when the Averages show signs of topping out. Or he may trade on individual swings, preferring, if possible, to sidestep the secondary reactions. In the latter case, he runs the risk of unloading at what appears to be a coming reaction, only to discover it is merely a decline or a period of hesitancy. There is much to be said for both schools; often the emotional make-up of the individual decides his course.

❦ ❦

Secondary reactions are, traditionally, the bane of the stockholder. Coming with little warning, they serve to correct the primary swings, as well as to dampen the enthusiasm of the amateur trader. They are caused by overspeculation and technical weakness in the price structure, or by the market's discounting a future business recession. Secondaries (often called intermediate reactions) tend to last from three weeks to three months, and to correct one-third to two-thirds of the previous primary advance.

In view of the losses which may be incurred during secondaries, the investor will ask, "Are there any signs in the Average which give warning of coming reactions?" The answer is yes. The same danger signs also may appear prior to mild declines or periods of hesitancy. For this reason, the secondary reaction is the most difficult single phenomenon confronting the Dow Theorist. Avoiding reactions always implies the willingness to pay the cost of "insurance," and greedy investors find this an almost insurmountable obstacle.

The danger signals of a coming secondary reaction include the following: (1) Volume becomes excessive (relative to that which preceded), with little or no movement in the Averages. (2) One Average declines persistently while the other advances. (3) Following a decline, an advance takes place in which one or both Averages fail to top their previous highs; the two then turn down and violate their previous lows on increasing volume. (4) One Average goes to a new high, but the other refuses to confirm. (5) Both Averages break a "line" downside (a line is a formation in which each respective Average remains within a 5% area for two weeks or longer).

As noted in previous articles, all extended bull markets have three phases. During the third or boom phase, the seeds of the next primary bear market will germinate. "It is in the third phase of a bull market that the most danger lies for investors because they (as distinguished from speculators) generally decline to practice the art of retreating when secondary reactions develop. Investors seem to prefer to sit tight on their holdings during these disturbances, and this trait tends to develop a false sense of security; they begin to think that each recession will be followed by new highs in due time, and that, consequently, recessions should be ignored. Ultimately such an investor attempts to ride through a decline which proves to be, not a recession, but the beginning of a primary bear market" (Rhea).

Perhaps the most common misconception about the Dow Theory is that it implies waiting for a bear signal in the Averages before selling. Nothing in the writings of Hamilton or Rhea remotely suggests such a dangerous method of operation. On the contrary, in 1937 Rhea observed that "It is my belief that the best market strategy for investors to study and practice is the art of retreating when secondary reactions are developing, and, as possible repayment for the time and effort involved, to profit, perhaps, through the replacement of their lines at prices below those existing when holdings were abandoned."

Bear signals may be recognized in the third phase of a bull market, as follows (see *Barron's*, Dec. 1, 1958): after a secondary reaction has been completed, an advance will take place. If one or both Averages refuse to better their previous highs, and the two then turn down, at the point where they both violate the lows of the secondary reaction, a bear market will have been signaled. After the bear signal, it will be necessary to reclassify the entire move. The reaction that appeared to be a secondary in a bull market now will be called the first leg of a new bear market.

It is much easier, in a bull market, to recognize the bottom of a reaction than the top of a rally. When a reaction appears to have hit bottom, Dow Theorists wait for the advance that eventually must follow. It is what happens after this advance that is crucial. If, on the next decline, one or both Averages hold above the previous reaction lows and volume decreases as these lows are approached, it is usually safe to say that the reaction is over. This, of course, implies that Dow Theorists cannot make purchases at the exact bottom of a reaction, and this is true.

This second decline wherein one or both Averages hold above the previous lows (as volume diminishes) is called a "buy-spot," and in the vast majority of cases these buy-spots work out well. Purchases are made in these areas on the premise that the next move will be up. A final penetration of the previous highs by both Averages simply will verify this bullish inference. In some few cases, buy-spots do prove false. Here the Dow Theorist finds himself holding securities which he purchased at the buy-spot, and after this both Averages violate their previous lows. The only thing to do in such cases is to jettison the recent acquisitions and pay the cost of "insurance" against a possible severe reaction.

While the Dow Theory can predict the direction of a move, it cannot predict duration or extent. Penetrations by both Averages through previous highs or lows are predictions of further advances or declines in the direction of the penetration, but the Dow Theorist knows that neither the timing nor the length of the move can be estimated.

Another important principle is that each successive penetration in a bull or bear market carries increasingly less validity. In a bull market, for instance, there finally will be a bullish penetration of previous highs, which should predict a further rise. But this will prove to be the last bullish signal prior to a bear market. Critics of the Theory then will claim that it does not work. They will disregard the many former bullish signals that were valid and point an accusing finger at the one that was not.

So far, most of our studies have pertained to bull markets. This is natural, since today we are in a great primary bull trend. Eventually, however, the tide must turn. It is therefore essential to know when and how this turn will occur. One of the first lessons to be learned from a study of the third phase of previous bull markets is that at such a time the arguments against the possibility of a bear market always run much the same. An impartial observer might conclude that it is not history, facts, or intelligence that guide most investors through the final phases of a bull market; it is hopes and wishes.

A sampling of quotations from newspapers and investment services taken near previous bull market highs furnishes dramatic proof.

A newspaper headline, which appeared two months before the 1896–99 bull market topp d out, proclaimed: "Bright Days for Trade—Proof of C owing Business on Every Hand."

One of the nation's largest investment services declared on Oct. 28, 1929: "The investor must have the picture clearly before him—and we must strongly emphasize this point—that the longer-range outlook is thoroughly promising. We therefore see no cause for alarm whatever for the investor."

A leading service announced, four days before the 1937 bear signal: "The worst we can see is a period of irregularity in industrial activity, possibily extending into the spring months. We do not believe this is the time to become bearish, or to throw good stocks overboard." The same service observed, a few days after the bear signal was given in 1937: "Retention of selected holdings in the more strongly situated industries is still fully warranted."

✾ ✾

Another well-known advisory service wired clients on Sept. 7, 1937: "Buy boldly." In the financial press, this organization announced, "Managed Money Has Made the Dow Theory Obsolete."

Still another service stated on Sept. 18, 1937: "Supply-demand conditions of business as a whole are unusually favorable. Business should rise sharply during the next several months." On September 25, another bulletin said: "Business activity will reach its low within the next week or two and will rise sharply during the remainder of the year." The market virtually collapsed during the next six months.

In view of all this, what can the investor and the businessman do to avoid the ravages of a bear market? In answer, Hamilton wrote, ". . . the stock market does predict. It shows us what will happen to the general volume of business many months ahead." But what of the managed economy, asks the investor, what of the safeguards, the S.E.C., the F.D.I.C., the Federal Reserve, margin requirements, Government spending? It is perhaps worth noting that the S.E.C. and the Federal Reserve were in existence in 1937, that margins were 100% when the 1946 bear signal was given, and that New Deal spending was considered shockingly large at the time of the 1937 crash.

Said Rhea in 1937: "Dow's Theory pays no attention whatever to wishful thinking of industrial leaders as expressed in bullish pronouncements; it makes little of Presidential scoldings. The primary trend of business and stock prices cannot be 'talked up' or 'forced down' by the President, by Congress, or by any single man or group of men."

꙳ ꙳

The next question, then, is, what to do when a bear market arrives? If the investor is out of the market or operating a short account, he should wait patiently until the primary trend runs its downward course. The value of his dollars, of course, increases as the market declines.

At some point, the Averages will have discounted the worst that is likely to occur. Here the Dow Theorist will seize another opportunity to buy.

At the bottom of a bear market, the news is usually most depressing. In 1932, for instance, many intelligent people firmly believed that the country would not survive. Stocks in the third phase of a bear market generally sell below their lines of value, or at liquidation prices. The market at the bottom becomes immune to the most shocking news, and the last decline usually is accompanied by very low volume (often about 10% of that which predominated at the bull market highs).

However, this final decline is not the buy-spot; it is merely the area at which Dow Theorists guess that the worst is over. Assuming that they are correct, an advance will take place. This could be either another reaction (upwards) in the bear market, or the first primary rally in a new bull market. The first decline following the rally should be scrutinized. If one or both Averages then hold above the previous lows and volume diminishes as those lows are approached, it will be the most bullish indication since the bear market commenced. Purchases here would be warranted on the assumption that the tide may have turned up.

The actual bull signal is given when on the second advance (preferably on increasing volume), both Averages top the highs of the first advance. This is the turn in the tide, and those who have not made purchases already should buy on the next decline that is accompanied by decreasing volume.

This whole procedure may sound simple and mechanical; it is not. For near the lows of a bear market little speculative cash is available. Stocks are out of favor and

the public is expecting worse to come. The analysts usually are advocating the utmost caution, and urging their
followers to avoid common stocks altogether.

Readers now may ask: "How accurate has the Dow
Theory been in predicting bull and bear markets?" The
history of its predictions is available at any large public
library. From Dec. 5, 1903, to Dec. 10, 1929, Hamilton,
the undisputed leader of the Dow Theorists during his
lifetime, called the turn in every bull and bear market.
His columns in *Barron's* and *The Wall Street Journal*,
are a matter of record.

Hamilton's single mistake occurred in 1926, when he
incorrectly announced a bear market during a particularly
severe and deceptive secondary reaction. He reversed his
decision a few months later. Perhaps Hamilton's greatest
prediction was his "Turn of the Tide" editorial which
appeared on the front page of the *Journal*, Oct. 25, 1929.
Here he called the end of the bull market in an unhedged
article, read by many and heeded by few. One month
later, he warned that ". . . those who look for a resumption of the old bull market may be assured that there is
not a single indication in the Averages that the decline
is over."

When Robert Rhea took over the Dow Theory, he
called the bottom of the 1932 bear market within a few
days. He successfully guided investors through the difficult 1932–37 bull market, announced the 1937 bear
market and the 1938 bull market, then died prematurely
in 1939.

But if the Dow Theory can call the turns accurately,
why doesn't everybody follow it? The answer is largely
greed, laziness, lack of knowledge, and wishful thinking.
When prices are advancing, the public, holding large

amounts of stock, wishes to be reassured. Investors like nothing better than bullish counsel during a bull market. Caution does not mix with greed, and the Dow Theorist grows cautious as the market climbs. As to ignorance, Wall Street is not immune. Moreover, it is easier to follow another's advice than to form one's own conclusion.

Lastly, the Dow Theory suffers from that prejudice which afflicts all technical market studies; it does not answer the question, "why?" The Dow Theorist has learned not to question the validity of a bear market signal which predicts a turn in the economy, nor does he deny the probability of an advance after industrials and rails better their previous highs. For him it is sufficient that the Theory has been tested and that it works. He knows that even if all the reasons for a move can be discovered, they invariably are learned after, not before, the move. The Dow Theorist has learned, in short, that it is better to leave the eternal question of "why" to the economists and the statisticians.

IV

Reading
the Charts

May 18, 1959

✻♫✻♫✻♫✻ Business throughout the country is excellent; it has been expanding for over a year. The sales manager of a large chain of retail stores notes, however, that sales have been sliding off at 15 of his 49 stores. He discusses this with the regional manager of 10 of the 15 stores in the afflicted area. The regional manager is well aware of what has been happening, but he is most interested to learn that this situation is extending to other stores outside his own territory. In fact, being a stockholder in the company the regional manager now decides to reduce his holdings. He sells 900 shares next morning at the opening, and the stock drops ¾ of a point; a single pebble has fallen in the way of the tide. That night the regional manager looks puzzled as he reads that the industrial average has dropped $3.00 during the day. "Strange," he muses, "I thought the market was heading up."

Because the stock transactions of the regional manager were duplicated by a hundred informed investors in other lines, the industrial average declined. This downward movement registered the sum total of hundreds of ideas, calculations, hunches, and scraps of inside information. Multiply this single movement through a series of ten or twenty trading days on the N. Y. Stock Exchange, and a distinct pattern will appear in the averages.

When a man places his money on a horse he does not change a hair of that horse's make-up; the horse performs the same regardless of whether there is fifty dollars or a king's ransom riding on his back. But every share of stock bought or sold has an effect upon the market; the investor's transactions are definitely registered in the price movements. Dow Theorists take this concept even further. They believe that the daily movements of the averages reflect the sum total of everything known by anybody which can possibly affect corporate profits and the general economy. Because of the unique nature of the averages, claim the Dow Theorists, the pattern formed by their movements is a prediction of things to come.

William P. Hamilton once remarked that the averages possess one property not shared by other prophets, when they have nothing to say they say nothing. And it is true that many of the fluctuations of the averages are minor or daily movements, which are meaningless for prediction purposes. But at other times the averages "talk"; when they do, it is in the form of a prediction. Many intelligent men base their business and investment policies on these periodic forecasts in the price movements; they follow the technical approach which says that the market is its own best forecaster. In the light of this it is interesting to follow the price movements of the averages through a complete bull and bear cycle. As the various formations present themselves, they will be analyzed and interpreted under the principles of the Dow Theory. On all diagrams, the top line represents the industrial average, the middle line the rails, and the bottom line the volume of transactions.

Diagram 1. The journey begins in the third phase of an extended bull market—a bull market that has been in progress for about five years. It has survived many secondary reactions, but following each of these reactions the averages have climbed to new highs. Volume is now clipping along at 3–6 million shares per day, which is perhaps five times that which was recorded when the primary trend first turned up. The public's interest in stocks is widespread; rumors, tips, and "inside information" are heard in every corner. Even the conservative investor who had faith only in cash and high-grade bonds now puffs his cigar nervously as he glances at the high-flying ticker tape. Perhaps he is buying common stock for the first time in a greedy attempt to make up for lost time and profits. The newspapers are glowing with bullish news concerning corporate mergers, sky-rocketing securities, new production records, and forecasts of even greater things to come. The crowd is buying with no regard for values as it pounces on the favorite stock of the day or hour. Inflation is rampant and money rates are high. Many of the leading economists are saying that there are not enough corporate shares to go around, and to remedy this situation, companies are issuing new equities as quickly as the market can absorb them. The average yield on the Dow-Jones industrials is 3.3%, and the low-priced stock indexes are higher than they have been at any time since the peak of the previous bull market.

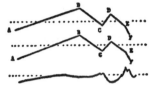

During all this excitement, the market has been advancing on the long swing from A to B. Volume has been increasing on this advance, but it levels off and declines near the peak at B. Subsequently both averages turn unexpectedly down for a period of three weeks to three months. On this downward swing, one-third to two-thirds of the previously uncorrected primary advance (A-B) is retraced. The duration and extent of this retracement classifies it as a full secondary reaction. The averages are saying: "If you did not sell on the previous rally, watch this move carefully. This is a secondary reaction in the third phase of a bull market. It could prove to be another reaction in a bull market or it could be the first primary leg in a new bear market." Following the lows of the B-C swing, the averages turn up and advance to D. Dow Theorists note that the C-D rally is steeper and faster than the B-C decline; this is not typical of bull market action. Volume on the C-D advance diminishes ominously, and the previous highs at B are not bettered by both averages. Here the averages say: "If you haven't sold already, you had better start selling now. Things are going to look very serious if a second decline approaches the reaction lows (C) as volume increases." On the next decline (D-F) the two averages gather momentum and violate the C lows at point E. "This is the bear signal," the market warns, "Forget all the bullish items you read in the newspapers, ignore what your optimistic advisors tell you, put your wishes aside. If you have not 'cleaned house,' do so tomorrow at the opening. The primary trend of stocks and the economy is pointing down."

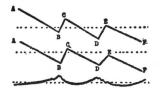

Diagram 2. A bear market is in progress. Dow Theorists have been the butt of endless "bear market jokes" because of their dire predictions made in the midst of an expanding economy. But since the bear signal, stocks have dropped sharply lower, and many portfolios already show large losses. Some analysts claim that the collapse is only temporary, that stocks cannot go down very far in the face of a "basically sound economy." There will be a resumption of the bull market, they promise, and stocks will climb higher than ever. Following the first primary bear swing (A-B) there is a rally (B-C), and here the public regains its old optimism. "I told you so!" laughs the bull as he calls his broker; he will pick up a few "bargains" in this area and average out his losses. But the B-C advance is a reaction (upwards) in a bear market; volume dries up near the highs (C) and Dow Theorists put out their first line of shorts. Because of the bear signal and because of the low volume at the highs (C), it becomes painfully apparent that both averages are not going to better their old bull market peaks. The market goes into another long decline (C-D), and it is now obvious that business, like the stock market, is worsening. The smiles are disappearing from the bulls' faces, and one hears of many large losses sustained by formerly wealthy stockholders. On each rally in the new bear market volume diminishes, following which the averages turn down and break their previous lows on increasing volume.

The current action of the averages is exactly the opposite of that which was seen during the bull market: the long plodding movements are downward, and the reactions (upward) are sharp and often violent. In the first phase of a bear market stocks sell minus the frothy "hopes and expectations" of the previous bull market's final boom phase. In fact, the bear market is now entering its second phase wherein securities discount a long period of progressively worsening business and a generally slumping economy. Many severe panics occur during the bear market's second phase, and support levels are swept away on the charts of individual stocks. News is disheartening now; one hears of dividend cuts, omissions, and pessimistic predictions of things to come. The economists are explaining how it all happened as the market continues on its ominous downward path.

Diagram 3. The bear market has been in effect for three years. This is about half as long as the entire preceding bull market. The stock market is out of favor, and one hears little of corporate stocks or even bonds. Unemployment is shockingly high, bankruptcies are commonplace, and some of the country's most respected institutions are reported to be in trouble. The "blue-chips," which had

held up better than most common stocks, have suddenly
collapsed in the most sickening fashion; many are selling
well below their accepted minimum line of values. "Good
stocks are worth six to ten times earnings," warn the

analysts, "and don't touch a stock unless it yields 6% to
9%. Let them pay you for taking a risk." A long list of
securities that were selling at 25–30 times earnings at the
top of the bull market are now going at ridiculously low
levels, and even at these levels there are few buyers.

A general air of hopelessness prevails, and many informed people believe that the country will not survive.
The market goes into another severe decline (A-B), but
there is something different about this new downward
swing—volume does not expand as prices fall. The market can, in fact, best be described as dull. Dow Theorists
are betting that the lows of the entire bear market are in
the making, this despite the fact that the majority of
people are convinced that business will be even worse
next year. A rally (B-C) ensues, and volume actually expands on the advance. Few people notice this phenomenon, for if the truth be known, few people are watching
the stock market at all. After the B-C advance the market
again declines, but this time volume diminishes sharply
on the decline. Dow Theorists are excited at this turn of
events. The averages are saying: "If on the decline one or

both averages hold above the previous lows at **B**, and volume diminishes as those lows are approached, it will be the most bullish indication since the bear market began." Dow Theorists decide that they will buy if one or both averages hold above the B lows on the calculated risk that the B lows represented the bottom of the bear market.

At D one or both averages hold above the B lows as volume diminishes. Dow Theorists close their eyes, disregard all the fearful news, and make their purchases. An advance (D-E) follows on which both averages better their previous highs (C) as volume bullishly increases. The averages say: "Your stocks were bought correctly at D. A bull signal has been given at the point where both averages bettered their previous (C) highs, and we are now in a primary bull market. Start expanding your positions on declines that grow dull, for the original primary bull signal is the most valid of the entire bull market." At this point, regardless of what the investor hears to the contrary, the averages are predicting better things to come. The time of increasing values has arrived, and a new bull market is born. But the vast majority of people are completely unaware of this important turn of events; they are still smarting from losses sustained during the previous bear market.

Diagram 4. Stocks are rebounding from the depressed levels of the third phase of the previous bear market. The averages are trending upward; each high bettering the preceding high (A-B-C-D) on both averages, while on declines one or both averages hold above the lows of the preceding declines. Volume is tending to expand on the rallies and diminish on sell-offs in typical bull market fashion. Advances are long and tedious compared to the sharp declines; this is action typical of a bull market. The newspapers are beginning to print mildly hopeful news

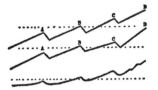

items, and a few people even venture the opinion that the depression cannot last much longer. Commodity prices are edging up and many "blue-chip" stocks have made rather significant advances. The public is still totally uninterested in the stock market; it always is during the first phase of a new bull market.

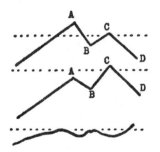

Diagram 5. Prices have advanced steadily for a number of months. The new bull swing has been uncorrected, and there is a tinge of confidence if not actual optimism in the air. Some of the large investors have bought heavily and they talk of riding the bull market to its eventual top. Others will attempt to avoid the first secondary

reaction in the hope of replacing their lines at lower levels. On the advance to A, volume has expanded bullishly, but near the highs it levels off and perhaps dips slightly. A minor decline (A-B) follows, and the trader is immediately on the alert. The averages say: "Watch the advance from B. If both averages better A on increasing volume the trend will continue bullish. But if one or both averages refuse to better A and they then turn down on increasing volume and violate the decline lows at B, this could be the beginning of a secondary reaction." On the B-C advance rails do better their former A highs, but industrials do not confirm the move. Volume has barely nudged upwards; thus two danger signals present themselves. Following the non-confirmation (on lower volume) both averages turn down (C-D) and abruptly violate the B points. Volume increases on the downward penetration. Many traders, noting the long uncorrected advance to A and the indecisive volume indications near these highs, have taken profits. Others took profits at C when it became obvious that industrials would not confirm the new rail highs. When the B lows were violated still others sold out. The large investor, on the other hand, has decided that he will ride out the reaction since he purchased his stocks correctly near the beginning of the bull market. He believes that the primary trend is still up, and he bases this on the fact that stocks are still selling on values; moreover, there have been no third phase characteristics in this bull market.

Diagram 6. The short-term sellers are correct. From the A highs the market begins a steady series of declines (A-B, C-D, E-F), each low on both averages violating the lows of the previous decline as volume picks up on

the downward moves. Stocks are falling much faster than
they advanced, which is typical of a reaction in a bull
market. The averages console: "If you still own stocks,
you will have to 'sweat them out'; they will come back in

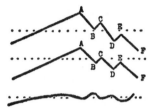

due time, and the reaction will not last forever." The
market is now showing the effects of too much company
on the bull side (it has been over-bought) or it is discounting an unforeseen recession in business.

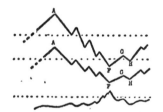

Diagram 7. The reaction which started at A has run its
course. The market has retraced about one-third to two-
thirds of its entire previously uncorrected primary advance; the downward swing has lasted about three weeks
to three months. It is a full secondary reaction, both in
duration and extent. At the lows of F (the bottom of the
reaction) a burst of volume appears; this is the selling
climax. But it is a very different picture from that which
was seen at the bear market bottom when volume dried

up on the final downward move (A-B on Diagram 3).
Dow Theorists do not buy at the lows of F, however.
They have guessed that point F represents the low of the
entire secondary reaction, but correct procedure tells
them to wait. Subsequent to the F lows, a rally (F-G)
takes place as volume bullishly increases. It is what happens after this rally that interests the Dow Theorist. Following the F-G rally another decline (G-H) takes place,
and on this decline one or both averages hold above the
lows (F) as volume decreases. At this point the Dow
Theory trader loads up with stock again; he has found
his buy-spot, and he is reasonably sure that the reaction
is over. The final confirmation of his bullish inferences
will come when both averages work their way up and
better the previous bull market highs at A. But the Dow
Theorist, as we have seen, does not wait for this confirmation; he has placed his orders on the expectation that the
final confirmation will occur.

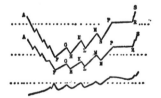

Diagram 8. Following the secondary reaction (diagram
7), the market moves between the reaction lows (F)
and the bull market highs (A). It is fluctuating in what
is termed secondary territory, and this is often a very
deceptive area. The climb back to the highs may be long
and tedious, unlike the violent descent which characterized the secondary reaction. Dow Theorists are studying
the action of the market carefully, and they are pleased

to see a succession of bullish signals (K and M, bettering of the previous highs by both averages) as the market works higher. Many formations which the Dow Theorist calls "buy-spots" appear on the rise. For instance, subsequent to the minor K highs a decline sets in. On this decline (K-L volume decreases bullishly, and one or both averages hold above their last minor low points (H). Stocks are purchased at L on the premise that the lack of selling pressure during the decline (K-L) is a bullish sign when coupled with the refusal of one or both averages to violate their previous lows (H). The two averages then advance and better the K minor highs. This bettering of K is a bullish indication and proof of the validity of purchases made near the minor decline lows at the buy-spot.

Just under the bull market highs of A both averages falter, then move sideways (P-R). Many traders believe that another reaction is forthcoming. But the averages are forming what is called a "line." They are fluctuating within an area of about 5% of their respective prices. The line is a formation wherein buying and selling are very evenly matched. If both averages better the upper limits of the line it will indicate that the buying (accumulation) within the line was better informed than the selling (distribution). If both averages penetrate the line downside it will mean that the sellers were better advised than the buyers. The longer and narrower the line (it must last at least 10 trading days to qualify as a line) the better the final prediction on the breakout. Both averages eventually break (R-S) the line topside (it is not necessary for both averages to penetrate a line on the same day, but the closer together the better the prediction), and the highs at A are finally bettered. It is a characteristic of lines that they possess more force on breakouts than do ordinary penetrations of high or low points. Lines often form just under areas of great resistance; they also occur in places where reactions might be expected. For this latter reason, many believe that lines may temporarily take the place of reactions in technically strong markets.

So far this article has stressed the implications of the movements of the averages themselves. It is extremely important, however, to remember that the Dow Theory concerns itself with many other aspects of the market. Dow and Hamilton, in fact, always attached the utmost importance to values. "Stocks fluctuate together," wrote Dow, "but prices are controlled by values in the long run." Again he observed, "The tendency of prices over a considerable period of time will always be towards values."

A study of market history reveals that the cycles of stock values tend to extremes. At the bottom of the 1932, 1942, and 1949 bear markets, the average yield on the Dow-Jones industrials was 10.3%, 7.9%, and 6.9% respectively. The bull market highs of 1929 put the average yield of the D-J industrials at 3.1%, 1937 at 3.7% and 1946 at 3.3%. It is obvious, then, that bull markets have usually ended when values, as measured by the average yield on the D-J industrials, enter a zone of about 3.5% or less. In 1902 Dow wrote, "When a stock sells at a price which returns only 3½% on the investment, it is obviously dear, except there be some special reason for the established price. In the long run, the prices of stocks adjust themselves to the return on the investment, and while this is not a safe guide at all times, it is a guide that should never be laid aside or overlooked." Dow's words concerning stock values have proved amazingly accurate as a guide for the investor who buys and sells values.

The degree of public participation and speculation have also proved helpful gauges with which to measure the market. Here is Robert Rhea's description of the great 1929 top: "All the usual indications of inflation were present. Volume of trading was excessive and broker's loans were making new peaks regularly—in fact, call money rates were so high that many corporations were finding it profitable to liquidate inventories and lend their cash equivalent to Wall Street at fantastic returns. Pool activities were being conducted on a disgraceful scale, brokerage houses were hanging out S.R.O. signs, and leading stocks were yielding less than the best grade bonds. Worthless equities were being sky-rocketed without regard for intrinsic worth or earning power. The whole country appeared insane on the subject of stock speculation. Veteran traders look back at those months and wonder how they could have become so inculcated with the 'new era' views as to have been caught in the inevitable crash. Bankers whose good sense might have saved the situation had speculators listened to them were shouted down as destructionists, while other bankers, whose names will go down in history as 'racketeers' were praised as supermen." During such times, it is obvious that, regardless of the fact that the averages may be indicating the continuance of a bull market, the end cannot be far off. Most Dow Theorists would gladly sell out of a market which has all the earmarks of a third phase climax; they never wait for the actual bear signal. Often, on the advent of a bear signal, stocks drop so fast that it is impossible to obtain quotes on securities. It is also possible that the actual bear signal will occur some distance after the pinnacle of the bull market. By the same token, Hamilton warns the investor not to rely solely on the Dow Theory to pick the bottom of a bear market. "No knowledge of the stock market barometer will enable any of us to call the absolute turn from a bear market to a bull market."

The test of a bear market bottom includes dull volume, sideways movement, immunity to bad news, and a general disposition among the public to expect worse things to come. In 1921 (September 18) only five points from the extreme lows of the historic 1921–29 swing, Hamilton applied the technical approach in connection with the price movements to call the turn. His prediction, which was worth a fortune to investors at the time, appeared in *Barron's*. "There is a pertinent instance and test in the action of the current market. I have been challenged to offer proof of the prediction value of the stock market barometer. With the demoralized condition of European finance, the disaster to the cotton crops, the uncertainties produced by deflation, the unprincipled opportunism of our lawmakers and tax-imposers, all the aftermath of war inflation—unemployment, uneconomic wages in coal mining and railroading —with all these things overhanging the business of the country at the present moment, the stock market has acted as if there were better things in sight. It has been saying that the bear market which set in at the end of October and the beginning of November, 1919, saw its low point on June 20, 1921, at 64.90 for the twenty industrials and 65.52 for the twenty railroad stocks."

Thus it can be seen that the Dow Theory is not merely a mechanical method for reading the averages. The Theory concerns itself with crowd psychology, volume of transactions, bull and bear market phases, degree of speculation, and all of these in relation to the action of the averages themselves. Many Dow Theorists use a variety of technical aids to measure the market's "psychology," and if used correctly these may be a definite help in applying the Theory. Some of these technical aids include the short interest, the short interest as compared to the average daily volume, the odd-lot indexes, the yield cycles of stocks, and the relationship of the Dow-Jones industrials to the low-priced stock indexes. While no single one of these indicators can present the entire picture, all of them used together may be of great help in judging the technical position of a bull or bear market.

V

Three
Major Tops

July 13, 1959

✳𝕁✳𝕁✳𝕁✳ The primary trend of the market turned up on June 13, 1949; it has remained up ever since. The phenomenon of a bull market lasting for over a decade, unprecedented in stock market history, has been instrumental in shaping the thinking of a generation. The opinion now is held widely that "inflationary pressures," "new scientific discoveries," "institutional buying," and "population trends" will insure a permanently high plateau for the American economy.

Many Dow Theorists, however, believe that the entire rise since 1949 will go down in the history books as part of a single bull market—admittedly greater in duration and extent than its predecessors, but in other ways quite similar. Furthermore, despite the predictions of the economists and money managers, Dow Theorists warn that

60

this bull market, too, eventually will top out, and that a new bear market will correct the entire rise since 1949.

❦ ❦

If the optimists are correct, then further study is unnecessary. One need only select a representative list of "sound" equities, lock them away in the family vault, and wait for profits to assume astronomical proportions. Yet on the Dow Theorists' assumption that the new "regulated" capitalism is still subject to cyclical swings and to the laws of supply and demand, a study of the final phases of previous bull markets may not be without value. The three major market tops of modern times occurred in 1929, 1937, and 1946; we propose to look at each of them in turn.

Many of today's 12½ million stockholders, it should not be forgotten, never have witnessed a major bull market top. The majority of those who have, probably were unaware at the time of what they were seeing. Basically, a top is an area of distribution and accumulation, but unlike most other bull market "congestion" areas, a top implies distribution by informed investors and accumulation by the public.

"Why do informed investors distribute at certain times?" readers may ask. The answer is that the market appraises and discounts the future. When experienced investors believe that stocks have advanced beyond all reasonable lines of value or when investors sense danger on the economic horizon, they will protect themselves by trading stocks for cash. The best atmosphere for such distribution is an optimistic one, in which the public will pay a premium for the investors' stock. Experienced market operators know that stocks are never cheap when the crowd turns bullish, and they often are willing to distribute their shares (which they bought at depressed prices) as the good news comes out. The seasoned investor then may wait months or years, if necessary, before entering the market again.

"It is much harder to call the turn at the top than at the bottom," wrote Hamilton, and the reason for this is logical. At the bottom of a bear market, it is readily apparent to informed investors that almost all stocks are selling below their lines of values; competition for securities is at a minimum, yields are high, and the public is disinterested. In such areas, careful and controlled accumulation takes place; the floating supply of stock is absorbed, and a long base is established from which the next bull market will rise.

At the top, however, price movements are erratic and often aimless. Informed distribution may take place at varying distances from the highs, and sometimes as much as a year away. Many stocks will not be overvalued near a bull market top; others already may have topped out. The general atmosphere will be one of excitement and confusion, with the public playing a major role, one which it never assumes at the bottom of a bear market.

Economic conditions vary and business procedures change, but the techniques of accumulation and distribution in the market remain much the same. The price movements at major market tops and bottoms, in fact, have traced remarkably similar patterns over the years.

Let us turn first to the late 20's. The years 1928 and 1929, as everyone knows, witnessed the most feverish stock speculation of the century. The U. S. had changed from a debtor to a creditor nation, and leading economists were quick to point out the bullish aspect of this switch. The Federal Reserve System was being held up as a bulwark against the type of collapse which had ended so many previous periods of economic expansion. Corporate earnings were increasing, taxes were being reduced, the nation's leaders were proclaiming a "New Era," and the vast majority of its citizens were convinced that good times were here to stay.

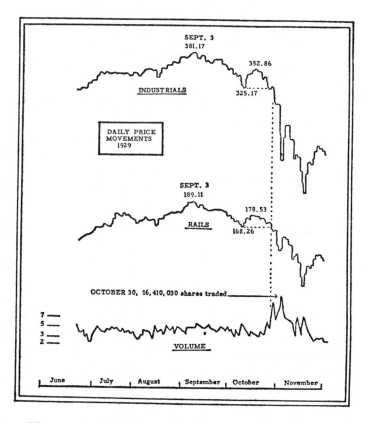

The market had been heading onward and upward ever since the recession year 1926. From 135.20 on

March 30, 1926, the Dow Jones industrials advanced to 322.06 on February 5, 1929. In an editorial in *The Wall Street Journal* on April 5 of the latter year, William P. Hamilton asked readers to apply the test of values to the market. "The student should ask himself if stocks are not selling well above the line of values, if people are not buying upon hopes which may be at least deferred long enough to make the heart and pocketbook sick." Hamilton's ominous query drew few replies. The public was far more interested in buying stocks than in answering academic questions.

From January through May of 1929 a long "line" (a period of evenly matched buying and selling) appeared in the averages; this area obviously was one in which informed investors were distributing their holdings to the crowd. It is common for the last line in a bull market to be broken on the upside, and 1929 was no exception. Following the breakout, another advance carried the industrial average to an incredible 381.17 on September 3, 1929 (see diagram 9). Rails on that day hit a high of 189.11, a level which has not been attained since.

ɷ ɷ

On the advance, volume averaged 4–5 million shares per day, a high level but still below that of the preceding swing, ended in 1928. Following the highs of September 3, a reaction lasting five weeks erased 56 points from the industrial average and 20 points from the rails. The move drew few comments from speculators. There had been ten other reactions since 1923, each followed by higher prices. Why should this one, they reasoned, be any different?

On October 21, 1929, however, Hamilton wrote an

article for *Barron's,* calling attention to this particular reaction. He noted the bearish implications of a swing which might take both averages back to, but not above, the previous highs, followed by a second decline which would violate the reaction lows. The reaction, observed Hamilton, already had lasted five weeks and had taken industrials from 381.17 to 325.17, rails from 189.11 to 168.26. Both in duration and extent, it qualified as a full secondary correction. On October 4, a second advance commenced, but this rally petered out in less than two weeks, both averages halting well under the previous highs. Following this second advance, the two averages turned down on October 23 and the lows of the reaction were violated decisively. This was the bear signal, which told Dow Theorists that the great bull market had ended at the September 3 highs. The "reaction" since those highs had been the first swing in a primary bear market.

On October 25, 1929 one of history's greatest stock market predictions appeared on the front page of *The Wall Street Journal*; it was Hamilton's editorial entitled "A Turn in the Tide." In a reasoned and carefully phrased article, Hamilton announced to an unbelieving nation that the tide had turned from bull to bear.

Four days later, on October 29, an incredible stock market panic exploded in Wall Street. The D-J industrials opened at 252.38, a full eight points under the previous day's closing! They then proceeded to drop 40.05 points during the day, before a rally temporarily halted the debacle. A few weeks later, the October 29 intra-day lows were shattered, and November 13 saw industrials close at 198.69, an unbelievable 182 points under the September 3 highs. Thus ended the first phase of the Twentieth Century's most drastic bear market.

Readers understandably may ask, "Why don't the experts recognize bear signals when they occur, and why do people hold stocks through bear markets?" One might as well ask, "Why do political leaders start wars, and why do men go off to fight them?" The answer, perhaps, lies within human nature itself; at any rate, bear markets and wars do occur. At sundown each day, every stock must have an owner, whether the primary trend is bull or bear. And just as buyers during bull markets hope that the rise is ahead, buyers during bear markets hope that the decline is behind. "It seems to take eight or ten years of familiarity with the price movements," wrote Robert Rhea in 1937, "for the average man to become convinced as to the futility of attempting to forecast the trends of business and stocks by studying such things as the current statistics of trade, production, etc., and, moreover, trying to combine these figures with estimates of the effect of war, social unrest, and a thousand other factors."

The bear market which began in 1929 hit its low on July 8, 1932, at 41.22 on the D-J industrials and 13.23 on the rails. These lows, though few suspected it at the time, proved to be the starting point for another extremely profitable bull market. The latter was to carry industrials to 194.40 in 1937 for a total gain of 372%, and rails to 64.46 that same year for a gain of 387%. The industrial percentage figure seldom has been equaled; the rail percentage, never.

Thus it was that the years 1936 and 1937 saw a great deal of renewed optimism. Stocks were headed sharply upward, corporations were prospering and the S.E.C. had instituted many regulations which were believed to safeguard against another collapse. The New Deal supposedly was "spending" the country out of the depression. The worst excesses of the 1929 period had been corrected, and it generally was held that "they" would not allow another crash to occur.

During September and October of 1936 Robert Rhea, successor to Hamilton as recognized leader of the Dow Theorists, warned that the market was entering its third and final phase. "Whether the S.E.C. can prevent the development of the usual exciting finish remains to be seen," wrote Rhea on September 5, 1936. "In my opinion it cannot."

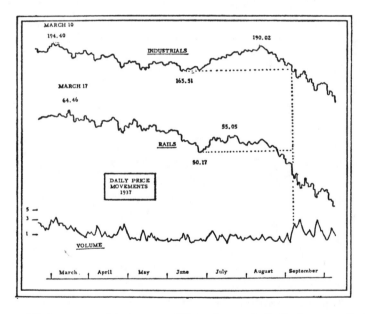

Volume was hitting 3 million shares daily in late 1936 as excited speculation enveloped the market. The "cats-and-dogs" were skyrocketing, the economy was booming, and on March 10, 1937, industrials hit a bull market high of 194.40. A few days later, rails hit their high of 64.46

(see diagram 10). Noting the sharp decline in Government bonds, Rhea wrote (March 24, 1937) of inflation and its accompanying dangers. "Politicians do not seem to grasp the fundamental fact that business expansion, rising labor costs, and speculation are blood brothers. When the demand is greater than the supply, both for labor and the products of labor, then prices of labor and 'things' advance; consequently people buy beyond their needs in order to avoid shortage or in the hopes of making speculative profits. The result is an expansion of industrial activity and profits which is reflected in rising stock prices—and the whole cycle makes people feel prosperous and happy. The last time I can recall official warnings from Washington designed to check speculation was in 1929. Then, as now, politicians seemed to think they could deflate the stock market, while permitting business to proceed with wide-open throttle."

❧ ❧

Rhea's words proved prophetic. Despite the prevailing optimism, the averages turned down from their March highs and embarked on a long decline which took industrials from 194.40 to 165.51 on June 14 and rails from 64.46 to 50.17 on June 28. From those lows, both averages rallied. However, in analyzing the price movements, Rhea warned that the rate of advance following the reaction lows was faster and sharper than the rate of decline during the reaction. This, he noted, was not typical of a bull market. Bull market advances tend to be extended and plodding, while reactions are usually violent and rapid. The converse is true during primary bear markets. Rhea also observed that the reaction was of sufficient duration and extent to qualify it as a full secondary. A bettering of the March highs now would be needed to reaffirm the bull trend. A violation of the June lows on increasing volume, on the other hand, would signal the existence of a bear market.

Volume on the rally which began in June dropped to less than a million shares per day. It was obvious that the averages would be unable to better their previous highs, and another decline soon was underway. On August 27, rails violated their reaction lows and on September 7 industrials confirmed that bearish signal. "This penetration," wrote Rhea, "interpreted according to the theory formulated in the last century by Charles H. Dow, means that the long bull market which started on July 8, 1932, terminated in March, 1937 . . . and that the movement since has been the first portion of a primary bear market."

The reaction to Rhea's widely quoted pronouncement was one of almost total disbelief. Business was excellent, and economists were offering bullish predictions of even better things to come. The investment advisors and brokerage houses were, in fact, more optimistic than at any time since 1929. Eleven days after the bear signal, Rhea wrote: "A friend suggested that I had better join the Chinese army if the averages prove to have given a false signal." The turn of events soon made a trip to the Orient unnecessary.

From the August highs of 190.02, industrials fell to 125.73 on October 18 without a single significant rally. The next day brought panic selling, as 7,290,000 shares changed hands. By mid-day the averages had dropped to an intra-day low of 115, but then came a recovery, which sparked an abortive ten-day rally. On November 20, 1937 the October 19 panic lows vere violated. The market hit bottom on March 13, 1938, at 98.95 on the D-J industrials and 19.00 on the rails. It had been one of the costliest and most violent bear markets in recorded history.

Rhea wrote the bull market's obituary during the fall of 1937: "Government with all its power can't control even the Mississippi River, much less the tides of American business or sentiment. Government money policies, if constructive, can help a bull market, but can't stop a bear market."

We come now to the bull market of 1942–46. This was a war baby, which began on April 28, with industrials at 92.92 and rails at 23.31. Taking the broad view, this bull market by its very inception predicted an allied victory in the war and the improved business climate to follow. By July, 1945, industrials had worked up to 169.08. Following a shallow decline, they commenced a new and impressive advance. Rails, having hit a high of 63.06 in June, dipped, then joined in the new advance.

Business was booming, the stock market was front-page news throughout the country, boardrooms were crowded, and the low-priced stocks were making spectacular moves. With war-time excess profits out of the way and a population starved for new products and consumer goods, it was reasoned, the stock market simply could not go down. By late 1945 the nation was witnessing another bull market third phase, much like that of 1936–37. The Federal Reserve Board had announced mandatory 100% margins on stock purchases as of February 1, 1946, and this action brought a torrent of buying by those anxious to capture their last bit of prosperity on credit.

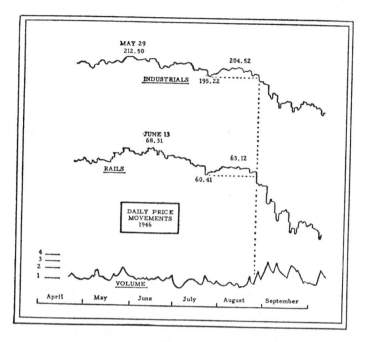

Informed investors undoubtedly sold on the upsurge that followed the margin announcement. On February 2, 1946, industrials hit a high of 206.97; three days later, rails hit their top of 68.23. The two averages then slid off in a sharp decline which ended in late February with industrials down 20.95 points (their biggest drop in the bull market) and rails down 7.70 points. This correction lasted three weeks and was of sufficient extent to be labeled a full secondary reaction.

Then came a surprising rally, which took industrials to new bull market highs of 212.50 on May 29 (see diagram 11). Two weeks later, the rails confirmed, in an advance which bettered their previous 68.23 highs by a scant eight cents! The continuance of the primary bull trend thus was verified. When new highs are registered by both averages, the significance of all previous points is erased. The market now looked ahead for clues regarding the primary trend.

❦ ❦

Volume had dropped considerably during the May-June advance, and many Dow Theorists took this as a danger signal. Immediately following the highs, the market went into a new decline. It hit bottom on July 23, at 195.22 for the industrials and 60.41 for the rails; the duration and extent of the move qualified it as another secondary reaction. A bettering of the May-June highs by both averages now would be needed to signal a continuation of the bull market.

Again the market advanced, but volume diminished pathetically (to less than a million shares per day) as prices worked higher. Three weeks later, industrials halted at 204.52, while rails fizzled at 63.12. Both averages had failed to better their previous highs. Dow Theorists were now on the alert, for any decline that violated the July 23 lows on both averages would signal a primary bear market. On August 14 the market headed down again, as volume expanded ominously, to over three million shares daily.

The "verdict of the market" was given on August 27. Both averages had violated their previous reaction lows and the bear signal told Dow Theorists that the action since June would have to be reclassified as the first leg in a new bear market. Those who made purchases on the basis of the June 13 rail confirmation (by the aforementioned eight-cent margin) failed to realize that the validity of upward penetrations in an aging bull market lessens as the market climbs. They ignored the fact that the D-J industrials in May, 1946, were yielding only 3.2%, that the bull market had lasted four years and had undergone all the classical signs of third-phase excess and speculation, that the low-priced stocks had risen to their highest levels since 1929, and that the majority of opinion held that the market could not go down in the face of the obvious prosperity. By October 9, industrials had dropped to 163.12; three days before, rails had hit a low of 44.69.

The S.E.C. later tabulated the literature sent out by 166 brokers and investment services during the week of August 26 to September 3, the very period when the averages were giving an orthodox Dow bear signal. Of 489 letters or wires sent out to clients, noted the S.E.C., 260 were extremely bullish, 97 were mildly optimistic, 74 advocated caution, 38 held no definite opinion, and only 20 (4.1%) were actually bearish and suggested at least some selling.

So much, then, for the record of three previous bull markets. In view of this recent history, one wonders if there is not a lesson to be learned. Perhaps the lesson was taught 57 years ago by Charles H. Dow, who warned investors to sell "when the bull chorus is loudest." Perhaps it may be found in Hamilton's statement that he had never known the majority of professional opinion to be correct.

This observer believes that if it is possible to learn from what has gone before, it might be summed up in the following paragraph by Robert Rhea: "Speculators who 'go broke' are usually those who fail to devote as much time to studying the subject of speculation as they do to the risking of an equal sum of money in their own business. These individuals will seldom admit that their ignorance is responsible for their losses. They prefer to accuse 'Wall Street' and 'bears' of having cheated them out of their money in some mysterious fashion. They fail to realize that no profession requires more hard work, intelligence, patience, and mental discipline than successful speculation."

VI

Tiring Bull?

September 28, 1959

✻∿✻∿✻∿✻ In an article in *Barron's* this past July, the writer ventured to question the thesis that inflationary pressures, new scientific discoveries, institutional buying, and population trends would insure a permanently high plateau either for the stock market or for the U. S. economy. In the short time since that article appeared, most stocks already have climbed down from the "plateau." Moreover, the recent action of the Averages suggests that an even more pertinent test lies ahead. Because this test will take place in the third phase of an aging bull market, it has a peculiar significance for followers of the Dow Theory.

Over the past 23 months, stocks have achieved an historic advance. This has taken the Dow-Jones Industrials from their October, 1957, low of 419.79 to an all-time

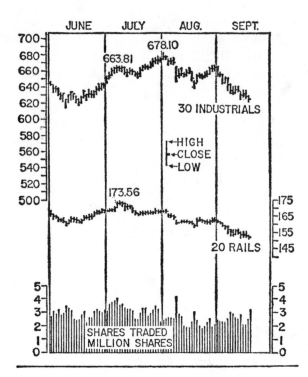

high of 678.10 on August 3, a gain of 258.31 points. The Rails have advanced from their December, 1957, low of 95.67 to a 1959 high of 173.56 (on July 8), a gain of 77.89 points. When an extended and uncorrected primary swing takes the market to new highs, and when the bull chorus sings loudest, Dow Theorists know that the next reaction cannot be far off. Such was the situation which prevailed throughout the spring and summer of 1959.

Under Dow Theory, for a bullish trend to be reaffirmed, both Averages must better their previous highs.

A movement of one Average unconfirmed by the other is useless for prediction purposes and, more often than not, deceptive. In the present market, the first danger signal began to flash after the last confirmed highs were registered by both Averages on July 8 (see chart). On that date, Industrials hit a peak of 663.81; Rails on the same day touched their high for the year, at 173.56. A minor decline ensued, following which another rally took Industrials to a new all-time peak of 678.10.

On this rally, however, Rails stubbornly refused to approach their previous 173.56 high. In short, the new Industrial high was not confirmed by the Rails. Subsequently, the latter turned down, violating their low of the previous decline. Three days later, on August 10, Industrials confirmed the Rail weakness by breaking through their own previous point of decline. Heavy volume accompanied the Industrial penetration, and the drop of 14.78 points was the largest single-day loss since the President's heart attack of almost four years ago.

Although this movement largely was ignored by the public, and even by Wall Street, a study of past price fluctuations suggests that the dual penetration should have been treated with utmost respect. The reasons are two: (1) it marked the first time since the October, 1957, bottom that both Averages had violated the lows of previous declines on high volume; (2) it came after an extended and uncorrected primary advance. The action of the market since the August 10 penetration has corroborated that early warning signal. Amid all the bullish news about spectacular corporate earnings, an expanding economy and a new capital goods boom, the two Averages retreated, in a series of sharp declines and minor rallies.

Industrials touched a temporary low in mid-August, then advanced sharply, and by late in the month had succeeded in retracing about half of the losses registered since the high. Rails, however, barely inched upward, again refusing to get "in gear" with the Industrials. It also is worth noting that the good volume which accompanied the June-July advance was not repeated on either the late July or late August rallies. Up to September 23, in fact, the action of the market has been impressive only on the downside. Following the minor peak of late August, the two Averages again declined. This time, Industrials violated all their lows since May, while Rails retreated to a new bottom for the year. By early September, it was obvious that for the first time since the 1957 lows, the secondary trend of the market had turned down.

In general, secondary reactions arrive when least expected and when the consensus is that lower prices are out of the question. In bull markets, secondaries serve the following purposes: (1) they may correct the previous primary swing and its accompanying excesses; (2) they may discount a forthcoming recession in business or a period of unfavorable news; (3) they serve to dampen the enthusiasm of amateur speculators; (4) they remind chronic bulls that the market can travel in two directions. In duration, secondaries tend to last from three weeks to three months; in extent, they tend to correct one-third to two-thirds of the primary swing since the end of the previous secondary reaction.

What often is overlooked is that serious reversals can begin in deceptively mild fashion. A few days in which the two Averages move in opposite direction, an unconfirmed high in one Average, perhaps a violation of the lows of the preceding decline on increased volume—any of these may mark the start of a secondary. As the reaction matures, however, there is often a period in which downward velocity increases, as stop-loss orders are set off and the fears of many investors are aroused. For this reason it is not unusual for the last day or so of a secondary to be accompanied by heavy volume, often termed a "selling climax." Yet every movement tends to overrun itself, and so it is with reactions. The market becomes oversold, the shorts hasten to cover, and the traders on the floor of the Exchange, sensing the (at least temporary) strength, jump in for the inevitable rally. It is the action of the market subsequent to this automatic rebound that is crucially important.

❧ ❧

Here there are two alternatives: (A) Following a normal correction of the reaction—say, an advance which retraces one-third to two-thirds of the ground previously lost—another decline will commence. If the factors responsible for the secondary are to continue or grow worse, the previous reaction lows are sure to be violated. Normally, this will produce an extension of the secondary. If this occurs during the third phase of a bull market, however, a primary bear signal will have been given.

(B) If the cause of the reaction has been discounted fully in the price structure, then on the second decline one or both Averages will hold above the previous reaction lows, and volume will contract sharply as these lows again are approached. An advance of both Averages over their previous highs then will signal a continuance of the primary bull trend.

The current downward swing may be taken as having

started on July 8, when both Averages established their last confirmed high points. Under this reckoning, a period of more than two months has elapsed. The time element, therefore, falls within that required for a secondary reaction. As of September 22, Industrials had retraced about 24% of all gains registered since the 1957 lows, while Rails had lost about 30% of their advance.

If this is to be a full secondary correction of the 1957–59 upswing, it is possible that the Averages will retrace the normal one-third to two-thirds of the previously uncorrected primary swing. Such a correction could take Industrials to or below 592 and rails to or below 147. Because of the extended period which has elapsed since the last confirmed highs, and because of the multi-stage pattern of the current downward swing, the correction so far can be taken as fitting within the definition of a mild secondary reaction. ❧ ❧

Under Dow Theory, the primary trend, once established, is taken to continue until countermanded by a valid reversal signal. Dow Theorists are aware, however, that any reaction in the third phase of a bull market might prove subsequently to have been the first leg of a primary bear market.

When the current reaction ends, if the two Averages rally and eventually top their previous highs of 678.10 and 173.56, respectively, the primary bull trend will be taken as continuing. If, on the other hand, subsequent to whatever secondary lows now are being established, the two Averages advance towards, but not above, the previous highs, the situation will be suspect—particularly if volume on the upswing remains low. Assuming an advance lasts a few weeks or more and retraces about one-third or better of the distance lost during the reaction, and that in a subsequent downturn both Averages break through their previous reaction lows on increasing volume, the primary trend may be considered to have turned from bull to bear.

VII

Tell-Tale Ratio

December 28, 1959

One of the tools which has proved valuable in appraising market trends is the short interest-average daily volume ratio (S. I. ratio). This ratio is obtained by dividing the total short interest on the New York Stock Exchange (issued every 30 days) by the average daily volume on the Exchange over the same one-month period. In May, 1931, the New York Stock Exchange began issuing weekly short interest totals; these figures were changed to a monthly basis in June, 1933. *Barron's* started publishing the S. I. ratio in 1947, and the accompanying chart shows the movements of this ratio, together with those of the Dow-Jones Industrials, from January, 1947, to the present.

According to the latest tally released by the N.Y.S.E. within the past fortnight, the total short interest dropped

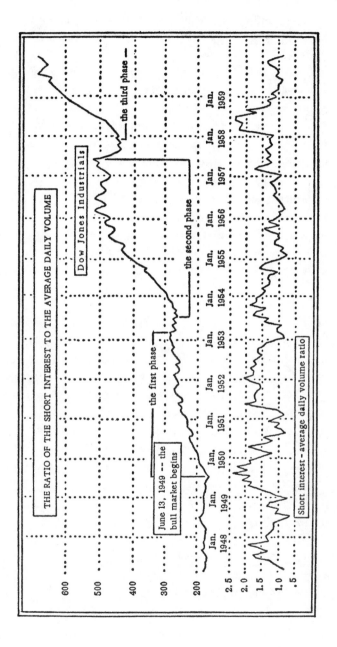

THE RATIO OF THE SHORT INTEREST TO THE AVERAGE DAILY VOLUME

Dow Jones Industrials

Short interest - average daily volume ratio

June 13, 1949 -- the bull market begins

the first phase

the second phase

the third phase —

Jan. 1948 Jan. 1949 Jan. 1950 Jan. 1951 Jan. 1952 Jan. 1953 Jan. 1954 Jan. 1955 Jan. 1956 Jan. 1957 Jan. 1958 Jan. 1959

600
500
400
300
200

2.5
2.0
1.5
1.0
.5

to 3,079,881 shares from 3,267,025 shares between mid-November and mid-December. At the same time, average daily trading expanded to 3,447,155 shares, from 3,291,669. As a consequence, the S. I. ratio declined to 0.89 from 1.01. In the past, the persistence of the ratio below 1.0 has indicated market vulnerability.

To see why, it is necessary to examine the influence of the short seller on the stock market. The short seller is actually selling shares of stock which he does not own (they usually are borrowed from his broker) in the hope of repurchasing these shares in the future at lower prices. His profit is the difference between the price at which he sold the borrowed shares and the price he must pay to buy them back, or "cover." Obviously, lower prices will provide profits for the short seller, while higher prices will produce losses.

❦   ❦

Every short seller directly affects the technical position of the market because, sooner or later, he is bound to cover his position. The short seller is speculating solely for the decline; he does not receive dividends (he actually must pay out dividends as they are declared), nor is he entitled to long-term capital gains on profits established through such operations. In other words, time is against the short seller—the longer he holds his position, the greater the financial and psychological handicap. This same principle does not hold true for the stock-holder who, theoretically, may hold his "long" position forever.

Often during a bull market an outside news event such as a war (Korea, Suez), a business recession (1957–58), or an unexpected news event (a Presidential heart attack) will cause a great many people to turn bearish and short the market (in complete disregard of the primary trend). In effect, these people have put out shorts in expectation of a severe reaction. However, in order for a reaction to occur—one great enough to be profitable for the shorts—there must be a heavy volume of selling.

If volume remains light, however, and if selling pressure does not materialize, the shorts are trapped. Traders frequently speak of a "sold-out" or "over-sold" market. In this case, they are referring to a market (usually a dull one) in which the worst already has been discounted. Put another way, prices have retreated to the "safety level," the bears have sold out and others have sold short. In such a situation, the amateur usually is surprised when, upon the issuance of the bad news, the market holds firm. In many instances, as a matter of fact, the market actually will rally in the face of the unfavorable news and, at such times, the trader is provided positive proof that fear-selling is over and that better things lie ahead.

All the foregoing brings us back to the S.I. ratio. We have seen that a large short interest constitutes a potential buying force in the market and that dullness during a bull market implies an absence of selling pressure. It follows, therefore, that the larger the total short interest and the lower the volume, the more pressure on the shorts. Such pressure builds technical strength in a bull market, which, in time, will force the shorts to "cover" their positions, or buy. It is this technical strength (or lack of it) that we attempt to measure with the S. I. ratio.

❦ ❦

Under this study, the technical condition of the market is taken to be strong when the S. I. ratio climbs above

1.5 and extremely bullish when the ratio goes above 2.0. A drop under 1.0 renders the market vulnerable, while a level of 0.5 or below definitely is bearish. The time element also is significant in connection with the S. I. ratio. For instance, the longer the ratio holds above 1.5 during a consolidation period, the greater the ensuing rise. Conversely, the longer the ratio remains in the 0.3 to 0.7 area, the more pronounced the technical weakness and the greater the possibility of a collapse.

Readers may observe that the S. I. ratio tends to climb during the early stages of important advances. Thus, in 1949, the country suffered its first post-war recession (many predicted a major depression), yet the Averages held within a narrow range as the S. I. ratio skyrocketed to almost 2.5. On June 13, 1949, the primary trend of the market turned from bear to bull, and the great "short squeeze" was on. From June, 1949, to January, 1953, the Dow-Jones Industrials rose from 161.60 to 293.79. By early 1953, however, the S. I. ratio had fallen under 1.0, and the first important reaction was about to occur.

During the business recession which followed the 1953–54 market drop, the S. I. ratio rose to almost 2.0. The bears (again expecting a collapse) put out their shorts against the primary bull trend. The S. I. ratio held above 1.5 for most of the latter part of 1953, a sign that the market was "sold-out" and strong technically. The Dow-Jones Industrials then began their historic second phase advance which took them from 255.59 in September, 1953, to a high of 521.05 in April, 1956.

The S. I. ratio dropped to the 0.8 area in March, 1956, foreshadowing the top which occurred a month later. Although working a bit higher, the ratio held below 1.2 throughout the remainder of 1956, as the Industrials formed a formidable double top (August, 1956). From this second top, the Industrials broke to 454.82 in February, 1957. The S. I. ratio, however, turned sharply higher in early 1957, hitting a peak of 1.75 in March. This short burst of technical strength took the Industrials to their famous triple-top of July, 1957. At the time of the '57 top, the S. I. ratio was back at 1.2, and from this area the July-October reaction took place.

The drastic late-'57 reaction caught the country by surprise, and once more the cry of "depression" was heard. But the S. I. ratio contradicted the almost universal bearishness by surging above 2.0 and remaining there for over four months. This was a phenomenon which had not been seen since 1949 when the primary trend was in the process of turning bullish. The great 1957–59 third phase advance drove 6 million shorts (the largest total in history) to the wall as the Industrials advanced from 419.79 to 678.10.

What of the erratic market of 1959? The S. I. ratio remained around 1.0 during the early part of the year, then advanced to an October high of 1.32. From October 15 to November 15 the ratio took a sharp drop to 1.01. The most recent figure—covering the period from November 15 to December 15—shows the ratio dipping to 0.89, its lowest point of the year, and, as noted, a possible indicator of market vulnerability.

If history repeats itself, we may expect a bull market top to appear when the S. I. ratio retreats to the vicinity of 0.5 to 0.7. At such a time, the average daily volume would be running about 40% to 100% above the total listed short position on the Big Board.

VIII

Critical Point

February 8, 1960

❊ᘓ❊ᘓ❊ᘓ❊ The puzzling behavior of stock prices in recent weeks once again has raised doubts in the minds of investors about the primary trend of the market. In the circumstances, a brief appraisal of the various swings of the averages since mid-summer, and what they might imply in the light of the Dow Theory, seems timely.

In *Barron's* (Dec. 1, 1958), the writer stated reasons for believing that the great bull market which began on June 13, 1949, was entering its third or "speculative" phase. In particular, the Dow Jones Averages had advanced all through the year without encountering anything more serious than a few minor declines. This unbroken rise was destined to continue until July 8, 1959, at which point the first signs of danger appeared.

The two averages halted (see chart) with Rails at 173.56 and Industrials at 663.10. A slight recession fol-

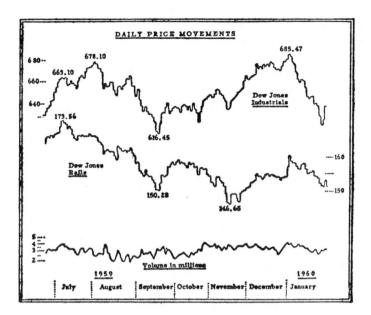

lowed, whereupon the Industrials alone rallied to a new high of 678.10 (August 3). The move, however, was not confirmed by the Rails. Under the Dow Theory, a penetration of one average not confirmed by the other is meaningless for prediction purposes, and, more often than not, proves deceptive. The deceptiveness of the August 3 Industrial high was soon apparent. Both averages turned sharply lower, and by September 22 the Industrials had retreated to 616.45, the Rails to 150.28.

❦ ❦

In the September 28 issue of *Barron's*, the writer called particular attention to this downward move. Readers were reminded that any reaction in the third phase of a bull market subsequently might prove to have been the first leg of a primary bear market. The article went on to say: "When the reaction ends, if the two averages rally and eventually top their previous highs of 678.10 and 173.56, respectively, the primary bull trend will be taken as continuing." But a note of warning was injected—if the two averages approached but failed to better their former highs, and ". . . in a subsequent downturn, both averages break through their previous lows on increasing volume, the primary trend may be considered to have turned from bull to bear."

A sharp rally followed the September 22 lows; then, toward the middle of October, a most unusual period of divergence occurred. While the Industrial Average worked higher, the Rails actually sank to a new low of 146.65. This Rail penetration was not confirmed by Industrials, however, the latter refusing even to approach their own low of 616.45. A bear signal thus was averted.

In late November, both averages finally got "in gear" on the upside, and an explosive rally resulted. January 5 saw the Industrial Average set a new high of 685.67. But once again the Rail Average failed to follow. Indeed, January found the carrier index lagging 13 points below its previous peak of July 8. A sharp decline began on January 6, and, in the space of eighteen trading days, almost all the gains since September were wiped out. In fact, last week saw both averages within striking distance of a bear signal.

Under the Dow Theory, a bull (or bear) trend continues until proved otherwise. However, if both averages now proceed to violate their previous reaction lows (Industrials 616.45, Rails 146.65), the primary trend will be pointing down. A bear signal, in turn, would mean that the bull market topped out on July 8, 1959, the day when the averages registered their last confirmed highs. It then would be necessary to go back and reclassify the July-September sell-off as the first leg of a primary bear market. The ensuing advance, which took Industrials to their January 5 high, would be the first reaction (upward), and the "reaction" since January 5 would be the second leg of the bear market.

Lacking confirmation by the averages, this writer makes no predictions as to the future trend of equities. In view of the prevailing uncertainty, however, it might be instructive to examine some of the all-but-forgotten characteristics of bear markets. "A primary bear market," wrote the great Dow Theorist, Robert Rhea, "is a long downward movement interrupted by important rallies known as secondary reactions. It is caused by various economic ills and does not terminate until stock prices have thoroughly discounted the worst that is apt to occur."

As is true in bull markets, most bear markets have three fairly recognizable phases. In the first, stocks sell minus the hopes and expectations which characterized the preceding top. In the second phase, stocks retreat in recognition of deteriorating business conditions and declining corporate earnings. This phase is marked by waves of panic selling. The last phase is liquidation, where good stocks are thrown overboard with the bad. In this final period, the majority of equities tend to sell below true values.

When the primary trend is down, the price movements are the reverse of those seen in bull markets. Bear market swings tend to be long and tedious, whereas rallies are sharp and violent. Following a reaction in a bull market, the averages usually move sideways for a time before starting up again; in bear markets, contrariwise, the primary downward legs frequently "turn on a dime," to be followed by explosive and deceptive rallies.

Hamilton noted that the old adage, "Never sell a dull market," was dangerous advice in a bear market. When the primary trend is down, dullness often precedes the next broad downward movement. Once such a swing is underway, volume again expands.

☙ ☙

A thorough understanding of volume indications and "crowd" psychology enabled Rhea to call the bottom of the 1929–32 bear market within a few days. On the final downward swing, volume usually remains low (suggesting a lack of distress selling), and the prevailing psychology is one of hopelessness.

Here is Rhea's description of the great bear market bottom (the final low came on July 8, 1932): "During June and the first half of July, the averages moved in a very narrow range, compared to preceding fluctuations. Volume was at a record low, considering total shares listed. Competent students of Dow's Theory generally recognized this action as the formation of a base for an exceptional rally. Many considered it the termination of the bear market, because past bear markets have tended to terminate with a sideways 'drag' on very low volume of trading after a long decline . . . During the six weeks ending July 15, prices had ceased to decline in spite of repeated shocks such as receiverships, important dividend omissions, the flight of our gold, the hoarding of currency, the bonus threat . . ."

The question most often asked during a bear market

is: "How long will it last and how far down will it go?" Students of Dow's Theory know that neither the extent nor the duration of a primary movement can be forecast in advance. In some bear markets, such as the one which took place between November, 1938, and April, 1939, the Dow Jones Industrials lost only 23.3% of their total value. Others, such as those of 1929–32 and 1937–38, saw Industrials lose 89.2% and 49.1%, respectively. An accounting of the fourteen completed bear markets since 1896 shows that the average percentage of loss in Industrials was 37.8%. In duration, the same fourteen bear markets averaged 512.8 days.

Comparative studies also suggest that the greater the duration and extent of the preceding bull market, the longer and more drastic the ensuing bear swing. Again, to judge by previous case histories, it may be said that most bear markets have retraced at least half of the total ground gained during the preceding bull market, while tending to last about 60% as long.

Since bull markets generally last longer than bear markets, it is readily apparent that price movements during bear markets must be more rapid. Interestingly, a detailed study of over thirty years of market action shows that during bear markets, the price changes are not only faster on the decline, but also on the rallies.

Contrary to popular opinion, finally, not all stocks collapse together in a bear market. Historically, low-priced stocks top anywhere from a month to a year ahead of the high-grade D-J Industrials, while many groups turn down well ahead of the actual bear signal. Edwards and Magee observe: "There were some important stocks that made their highs long before the 1929 top. Chrysler, for example, made its high in October, 1928, and had dropped from 140 to 60 before the panic of 1929 . . . By actual count of nearly 700 listed stocks, 262 issues made their bull market highs before 1929, 181 topped in 1929, but before August of that year."

IX

Bear Market
Signalled

March 7, 1960

❦♪❦♪❦♪❦ On March 3, 1960, the twenty stocks which constitute the Dow-Jones Rail Average closed under their November low. This move confirmed the February 16 penetration by Industrials through their respective September low. According to the classic theory formulated by Charles H. Dow at the turn of the century, the two Averages thus have given the signal for a bear market in stocks. This means that the great bull market which began on June 13, 1949, ended on July 8, 1959. The movements since then have been part of a bear market (see *Barron's*, Feb. 8, 1960).

A study of history shows that the primary and secondary swings of the stock market serve to discount forthcoming periods of expansion and contraction in the economy. While no one can predict the duration or extent of a primary movement, it should now be recognized that Dow's Theory has sounded its gravest warning.

Since the beginning of 1960, we have witnessed the phenomenon of a market which has ignored both the forecasts and the forecasters. To the causal observer it may well seem that the market has "taken leave of its senses." Yet there is nothing new in a stock market which will not perform as it is "supposed to." William P. Hamilton, the great editor of *The Wall Street Journal*, perhaps explained this best when he wrote: "The market has often seemed to run counter to business conditions, but only for the reason that represents its greatest usefulness. It is then fulfilling its true function of prediction. It is not telling us what business is today, but what the future course of business will be."

Many of today's investors have never seen the turn of an extended bull market, yet the dynamics of the reversal have remained the same through the years. Following a reaction in the third or speculative (bull market) phase, one or both Averages approach but fail to better the preceding highs on the ensuing advance. If on a subsequent decline, both Averages then break their reaction lows, the primary trend is considered to have turned from bull to bear. That is now the case.

X

Deceptive Rallies

May 16, 1960

✻♪✻♪✻♪✻ On March 9, 1960, one week after the Dow Theory bear signal was given, the two Averages turned sharply upward (see chart) and a rally was underway. The advance ended for the Rails on March 24 at 146.56, for the Industrials on April 18 at 630.77. In duration the rally lasted six weeks; in extent it corrected 37% of all losses (on both Averages) sustained since the highs on January 5. Since a secondary reaction by definition is an important movement, lasting approximately three weeks to three months, and tending to correct one-third to two-thirds of the previous primary swing, the March-April advance qualified as a secondary reaction in a bear market.

"An understanding of secondary reactions," wrote the great Dow Theorist, Robert Rhea, "is needed by traders to about the same extent as a growing cotton crop requires sunshine." Yet the secondary reaction is probably the most perplexing phenomenon with which the average investor must contend. Perhaps this article may shed some light on a complex and badly understood subject.

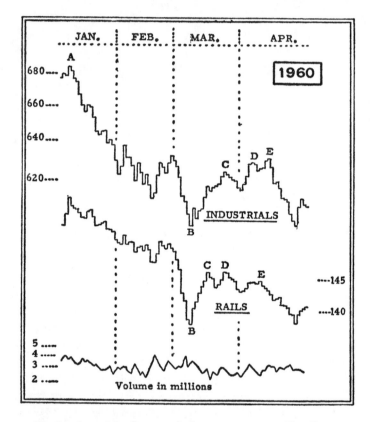

To begin with, let us define our terms. Readers are aware that a bull market leg (swing) is a broad upward movement of stocks, while a bull market reaction is an important decline against the primary trend. However, since under the Dow Theory a bear market is now in progress, one must reverse the terminology. In bear markets the primary legs are downward, while the secondary reactions, or rallies, are upward movements against the prevailing primary trend.

Every bear market is made up of two or more downward legs (primary swings) and at least one secondary reaction. Some bear markets, such as that of 1909–1910, were confined to the minimum. Others, such as the bear market of 1919–21, had six primary legs and five secondary reactions. The great 1929–32 affair was made up of no fewer than eight distinct primary legs and seven secondaries, a series which has not been matched before or since.

"Secondary reactions," wrote Rhea, "are as necessary to the stock market as safety valves are to steam boilers." In other words, when the stock market steam engine is straining, and too many passengers have climbed aboard, the safety valve (secondary reaction) is released. Although many reasons are given for every move of this kind, it may be said that all secondaries serve the following purposes: (1) to correct a primary market movement which has gone too far in one direction; and (2) to dampen the speculative ardor of the amateur trader.

Despite their importance, most investors have great difficulty in recognizing the advent of secondary reactions. "It may be conceded at once," wrote Hamilton, "that if it is hard to call the turn of a great bear or bull market, it is still harder to say when a secondary movement is due . . ." To compound the hazards, secondaries often are mistaken for a true reversal of the primary trend. In bear markets, stockholders are anxiously awaiting the return of the bull tide; they are eager to seize upon any rally as the "turn."

In bull markets most reactions end with a day or so of heavy volume, a characteristic which can be of real use in identifying the bottom. But a primary leg in a bear market may or may not end on heavy volume. Thus the termination of a bear market leg, and the beginning of a rally, cannot always be spotted by volume indications alone. However, it often happens that after an extended bear market decline, there will be a day or two of high volume. If the decline then continues, but volume shrinks drastically, the odds favor an early reversal.

Moreover, while the precise turning point is difficult to recognize, the price movement itself, after a long decline, may give significant indications of an impending rally. These signs are described by Rhea: "A study of secondary reactions in bear markets will reveal the fact that the development of those movements is usually indicated by a series of minor rallies and declines, with each rally generally carrying above the preceding one, and declines terminating above immediately preceding lows. Such a formation in the averages forecasts a secondary advance, even though the primary trend is down." It should be remembered, however, that both Rails and Industrials must confirm in such a movement before valid inferences can be drawn.

Reactions (whether in bull or bear markets) nearly always consume less time and are more violent than are the movements in the direction of the primary trend. It is not unusual, in fact, for a three-week rally in a bear market to retrace 30% to 60% of a downward swing which may have taken many months to complete. "It is a tried rule, which will help to guide us in studying the secondary movements, that the change in the broad general direction of the market is abrupt, while the resumption of the major movement is appreciably slower." (Hamilton)

Following a reaction in a bull market, a base is formed at or near the reaction lows, and it may take weeks or even months of accumulation before stocks then begin the next bull swing. The explanation is simple: after a bull market reaction, investors begin accumulating stocks, and this accumulation is carried on as close to the lows as possible.

Bear market secondaries, in contrast, often present a "bouncing" or "turn on a dime" appearance; the rallies seem to spring from no visible base or area of support. Again the cause is evident. Bear market reactions invariably result from a technical condition in which the market becomes "over-sold." The turn to the upside may be set off by professional short sellers who realize that the time has come to cover. Amateur short sellers, having made their move too late, quickly follow the professionals' lead. Floor traders, sensing the reversal, throw the weight of their buying behind the market. Thus the rally is on. Obviously, such a phenomenon is not a forecast of a fundamental turn, but is merely a technical rebound in a market that has gone too far and too fast.

It is invariably easier to call the end of a bear market rally than the beginning. Rhea described one of the best methods for identifying the top. "In such action the peak is frequently attained on a sudden increase in activity lasting a few days. It is usually impossible to pick the turn with any degree of precision; however, if, after the high point has been attained, a further rally shows a definite diminution in activity, it is probable that an early resumption of the decline will occur."

Dullness following the peak of a bear market rally is a common danger sign. However, it is often confusing to the average investor, who fails to realize that the old adage, "Never sell a dull market," does not apply when the primary trend is down. Dow was the first to recognize the implications of dullness. In 1902 he wrote: ". . . the action of the market after dullness depends chiefly upon whether a bull or a bear market is in progress. In a bull market, dullness is generally followed by advances, in a bear market by declines." He adds that in bear markets ". . . prices fall because values are falling, and dullness merely allows the fall in values to get ahead of the fall in prices."

Following a bear market rally, one Average often advances to a new high, but this high may not be confirmed by the other Average. In such areas dullness often occurs, after which both Averages sag below preceding decline points, and the primary downtrend again is resumed.

Psychology during bear market rallies seems to follow a fairly consistent pattern. "During secondary reactions in bear markets," wrote Rhea, "it is a fairly uniform experience for traders and market experts to become very bullish. They usually are bearish about the time the upturn comes."

The converse holds true of the psychology which precedes a bear market rally. Here, boardroom "oracles" are gloomy, investment services are pointing out the advantages of bonds and "defensive stocks," and neophytes are trying their hand at shorting. The bad news, which already has been discounted in the downward swing, is appearing on all sides. At such times, a bear rally is in the making.

Since January, this classic pattern has repeated. A primary bear market leg (A-B, see chart) hit bottom at B. From this point, a typical bear market reaction then ensued. The Averages rallied sharply, seeming to "turn on a dime." Rails established their rally high points quickly at D; Industrials, however, built a more impressive structure, with successive highs at C, D and E. But at E the Rails refused to confirm.

Shortly afterward, the Rails turned sharply lower, and this time Industrials declined in sympathy. Preceding minor decline points were violated and, as the B lows again were approached, the action became erratic, with both Averages rallying for a day or so before retreating.

This is how matters now stand. A joint violation of the B lows (Rails already have done so) will signal that a new primary bear leg is underway. However, if the Industrials can hold above their low (599.10), and if, in a subsequent advance, both Averages manage to better their preceding secondary highs (Industrials 630.77, Rails 146.56), the secondary trend will be considered as remaining up.

XI

Downturn Confirmed

September 26, 1960

🎵🎵🎵🎵 During the past six months, the Dow Jones Averages have been weighing prospects for business with cold objectivity. Last week, when the two indicators plunged to new lows, the not-so-bloodless verdict was handed down. The Averages, interpreted under Dow's Theory, have said that business conditions will worsen over the foreseeable future. The bear market signal, first given in March, has been confirmed.

On March 7, 1960, the writer stated in *Barron's* that under orthodox Dow Theory, the primary trend of stocks and the economy must be considered to have turned from bull to bear. He went on to say, "While no one can predict the duration or extent of a primary movement, it should now be recognized that Dow's Theory has sounded its gravest warning."

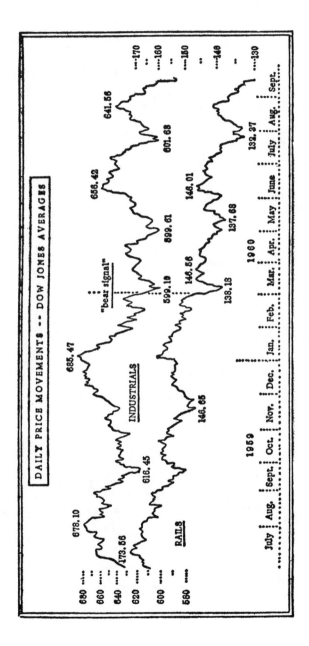

DAILY PRICE MOVEMENTS -- DOW JONES AVERAGES

On March 8, Industrials dropped to a low of 599.10, Rails to 138.18. An extended and complex secondary reaction (rally) followed, which took Rails to a secondary high of 146.56 on March 25, Industrials to a secondary peak of 656.42 on June 9. During this rally, it is worth recalling, security analysts and much of the financial press conducted a running debate regarding the validity of the bear signal, as well as that of the Dow Theory itself. Most observers embraced the view that the decline was merely a "shakeout," preparatory to new highs in the Averages.

During the period following March 8, the Rail Averages twice broke into new low ground. On May 10, Rails sank to 137.68; on July 27, a further low of 132.37 was recorded. Over the same period, a so-called "triple-bottom" was formed by the Industrial Average, with lows of 599.10 (March 8), 599.61 (May 2) and 601.68 (July 25). Despite an equally impressive series of descending Industrial peaks, 685.47 (January 5), 656.42 (June 9) and 641.56 (August 24), the "bullish import" of the triple-bottom was widely proclaimed.

❦ ❦

In this connection, it is worth noting that the great Dow Theorist, William P. Hamilton, attached little significance to "double" or "triple" tops or bottoms. Regarding double bottoms, Robert Rhea, leader of the Dow Theorists during the 'thirties, wrote: "It would be interesting to know who was first responsible for convincing the public that such phenomena formed an integral part of the Dow Theory." Rhea added: "Any student making a painstaking analysis of the subject is certain to concede that inferences drawn from the theory of 'double tops' and 'double bottoms' are more apt to be misleading than helpful."

The recent action of the market would seem to bear out these views. On Sept. 15, 1960, the Rails violated their preceding low of 132.37. Three trading days later, Industrials confirmed by violating their bear market low of 599.10 (recorded on March 8). The heaviest volume in three months accompanied the penetration of the widely-heralded triple-bottom. Since both Averages penetrated their lows within the short span of three trading days, accompanied by heavy volume, Dow Theorists felt that the movement commanded added authority. The primary trend or great tide of the market has been reconfirmed as being downward.

In the brief article entitled "Bear Market Signalled," last March, the following statement was made: "A study of history shows that the primary and secondary swings of the stock market serve to discount forthcoming periods of expansion and contraction in the economy." Accordingly, it is interesting to follow the trend of *Barron's* own Index of Business Activity during recent months. In January *Barron's* Business Index touched a high of 106.6. In the week of March 7 (the week of the bear signal), the Index stood at 101.4. By last week, however, it had dropped to a low of 80.3. In short, as measured by *Barron's* Index, business activity is now 27% below its January high point. Moreover, 80% of the drop came after the bear signal.

A widespread misconception exists regarding news and its effect upon the market. Last week's break, for instance, was widely blamed on poor corporate statements, bearish "talk" and an inundation of "Iron Curtain" visitors to the United Nations. It should be recalled, however, that the market acts not upon the news of the day, but on what can be seen ahead by the combined intelligence of all investors everywhere. Thus the lows of March 8, 1960, discounted all the disappointments which have materialized over the past six months. By the same token, last week's new lows are a prediction of further difficulties which may not appear for perhaps weeks or months from now.

As described in previous articles, bear markets generally have three psychological phases. In the first, stocks sell minus the "hopes and expectations" of the previous bull market. During the second (and usually the longest) phase, stocks go down in response to shrinking corporate profits and deteriorating business conditions. This phase is distinguished by occasional panics and sudden sharp breaks in individual stocks. In the third phase, stocks retreat below accepted or known values; it is here that equities are sold because investors want to raise cash or conditions seem hopeless. To judge by the behavior of stocks last week, the bear market now has entered its second phase.

At the same time it also has launched upon its third primary leg. This is an actual price movement, which should not be confused with the psychological phases cited above. All bear markets have at least two primary (downward) legs and at least one (upward) reaction. The greatest number of primary legs ever recorded in a bear market, that of 1929–32, was eight. It is a characteristic of both bull and bear markets that movements in the primary direction tend to be long and plodding, while reactions are violent and sharp.

The first primary leg of the current bear market started

for Industrials on Aug. 3, 1959, at 678.10, and ended on September 22 at 616.45. The second began on Jan. 5, 1960, at 685.47, and ended on March 8 at 599.10. The third leg began on June 9 at 656.42, and, at this writing, is still underway.

Dow's Theory states that neither the duration nor extent of a primary leg can be predicted in advance. This principle applies right now. When primary points (in bull or bear markets) are jointly penetrated, the significance of all preceding levels is erased. Therefore, as far as Dow Theorists are concerned, the current downswing is subject to no important "resistance levels" or previous lows. The market is a law unto itself, and during primary movements, past experience suggests the wisdom of avoiding preconceived ideas.

What is plain is that sooner or later there will be an upward correction or reaction. This rally in all likelihood will retrace the normal one-third to two-thirds of whatever losses are sustained on the current leg down. Moreover, while any advance conceivably may be the start of a new bull market, neither the length of time elapsed, phase, volume, investor psychology nor current stock values suggest that a bear market bottom is close at hand.

XII

Will History
Repeat?

December 19, 1960

✳♪✳♪✳♪✳ A great deal of comment has arisen as
to whether the current bear market is not merely "another 1957-type reaction." Wall Street, which is understandably committed to the "constructive" side, has
always been influenced in its thinking by the events of
the most recent past. "The Street" remembers that Industrials "topped" in July, 1957, following which, the
senior Average dropped 100 points to establish a final
low in October of that year. Then, despite the deepening
business recession (which did not touch bottom until
April, 1958), the Industrial Average entered upon a long
sidewise movement preparatory to the explosive third
phase advance of 1958–59. That advance predicted the
forthcoming economic upturn, an upturn which was not
apparent until the latter part of 1958.

The bear market which began in July, 1959, has (so far) erased 119 points from the peak price of the Dow Jones Industrial Average and 53 points from the peak price of the Rail Average. This erosion has taken place over a period of fifteen months. From the standpoint of timing, the current bear market is in stark contrast with the reaction of 1957. At that time the Industrial Average lost 100 points within a period of three months. Preceding articles in this series have stressed the fact that primary movements tend to be long and plodding, whereas secondary reactions (against the primary trend) tend to be short and violent. Most secondary reactions last from three weeks to three months, a time span which would easily encompass the decline of 1957. Unfortunately, the broad decline which began in 1959 allows of no such classification.

While the current decline could conceivably turn out to be a repeat of 1957, there are certain fundamental differences in the markets of 1957 and 1959–60 which are well worth noting. The contrasting element of timing has already been mentioned. In order to examine a few of the other differences, it is necessary to turn to the philosophy and theory of Charles H. Dow.

To many, Dow's Theory is a simple trend analysis system; one observes the pattern of the Averages and becomes bullish or bearish depending upon whether the indicators penetrate preceding highs or lows. Nothing could be further from the truth. It is well to remember that the movement of stocks is always an effect, never a cause, and simple conclusions based on a *mechanical reading* of the Averages are liable to be both deceptive and costly.

Dow attached great importance to the study of *values,*

as well as to the trend of the market. This emphasis on values is evident from even a cursory reading of Dow's original *Wall Street Journal* editorials. A few excerpts from those editorials follow:

> "The first thing for any operator to consider is the value of the stock in which he proposes to trade. The second is to determine the direction of the main movement of prices."

> "Stocks fluctuate together, but prices are controlled by values in the long run."

The following two quotes contain material of far-reaching importance:

> "We have tried to show . . . that value has little to do with temporary fluctuations in stock prices, but is the determining factor in the long run. Values, when applied to stocks, are determined, in the end, by the *return to the investor*, and nothing is more certain than that the investor establishes the price of stocks."

> "When a stock sells at a price which returns only about 3½ per cent on the investment, *it is obviously dear*, except there be some special reason for the established price."

In other words, Dow believed that "the return to the investor" or yield was a critical test of value. Secondly, he believed that when a stock yielded "only about 3½ per cent" it had reached the point of over-valuation.

Keeping Dow's concept of values in mind, the writer

has made a careful study of the average yield on the D-J Industrials from the 1920's to the present. This study suggests the following: (1) the average yield on common stocks (i.e. the D-J Industrials) is subject to wide and extended swings. These swings coincide with the progress of major bull and bear markets. (2) Investors tend to distribute stocks when those stocks become overvalued (or when the average yield on the D-J Industrials

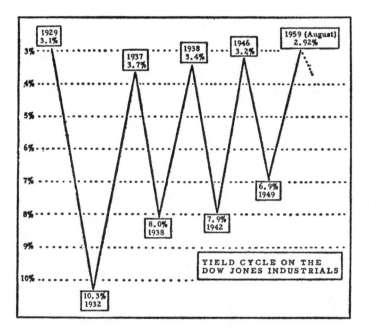

recedes to the 3½% area). Investors tend to accumulate stocks when those stocks become under-valued (or when the average yield on the D-J Industrials rises above the 6% area).

Judged in the light of thirty-five years of market history (see chart of the yield cycle), Dow's original ideas concerning yield and values have proved remarkably correct. Consciously or unconsciously, investors tend to accumulate or distribute stocks within broad areas of under-valuation or over-valuation. These areas correspond to the formation of bear market bottoms and bull market tops.

The accompanying yield cycle chart shows the major swings of yields since 1929. The "New Era" bull market of the 1920's expired in September, 1929, with the average yield on the D-J Industrials at a low of 3.1%. The aftermath of the speculation of the '20's was the worst bear market in recorded history. By 1932 the average yield on the Industrials had increased to a depression high of 10.3%.

On July 8, 1932, a new bull market began, a bull market that was destined to quintuple the price of the D-J Industrials in the next five years. At the peak of the new bull market (1937) yields again entered the over-valued area, this time at 3.7%. By 1938 a drastic one-year bear market had returned yield to 8.0%. An extremely short bull market reduced average yields to a dangerous 3.4% later that year, and this was followed by the 7.9% yields which accompanied the extreme bear market lows of April, 1942.

The bull market of 1942–46 was a "war baby," but the war and its aftermath did not stop yields from touching 3.2% in 1946. From here yields increased steadily as stocks sank to their bear market lows of June, 1949. In 1949 the average yield on the D-J Industrials rose to 6.9%, and from this base of accumulation the bull market of 1949–59 was born. Over a ten year period yields slowly diminished, so that by July, 1959, the average yield

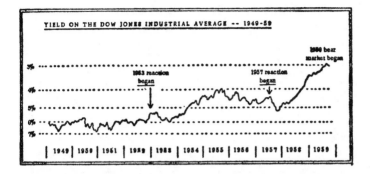

YIELD ON THE DOW JONES INDUSTRIAL AVERAGE -- 1949-59

on Industrials had dropped to an incredibly low 2.92%.

The second yield chart shows (in detail) the progress of Industrial yields through the 1949–59 bull market. Note that during the years 1949 to 1952 the average yield on the Dow stocks held in the under-valued 6–7% range. Since investors appreciate values, it is apparent that this was the area in which the important accumulation of stocks took place.

In 1953 the yield cycle reached 5¼%, and it was here that a severe secondary reaction occurred. Many investors were quick to cry "bear market," but judging by average yields the bear market premise was at best highly questionable. The yield cycle in 1953 suggested (1) that stocks were still values, (2) that no important distribution had taken place.

From 1954 to 1957 average yields held in the 4–5% range, and here again there was no suggestion (from the standpoint of values) that a bull market top had formed. By 1957 the bull market was six years old, *yet yield had never dropped to anything like the over-valued situation which existed in 1929, 1937 and 1946.* For this reason the 1957 drop was not taken (at least by this observer) to be the beginning of a major bear market.

In late 1958 (see "Dow Theory Revisited, *Barron's*, December 1, 1958) for the first time during the life of the great bull market, yields dropped into the 3½% zone. Such over-valuation taken together with other bull market third-phase characteristics implied that a period of major distribution was developing. Of interest is the fact that *from late 1958 to the present,* the average yield on the thirty Dow Jones Industrial stocks remained in the 2.9 to 3.8% area. This represents the longest period of common stock over-valuation in market history.

Another important factor in gauging the phase of a bull market is the action of low-priced stocks. A study of market action since the turn of the Century shows that during the third or final phase of each major bull market, the low-priced stock (or "cats-and-dogs") undergo excited and often spectacular advances. As early as 1899 (near the peak of the 1896–99 bull market), Dow called his readers' attention to the movements of the low-priced stocks (called "fancy stock" in those days): "Just at present there is a perceptible increase in trading in fancy stocks. This has not always been the best sign of a continued general upward movement for any great length of time, although it is certainly an accompanying feature of a bull market."

Thirty-seven years later Robert Rhea commented on low-priced stock action during the third phase of the 1932–37 bull market: ". . . this is the phase where worthless stocks are bought for no other reason than because they look cheap, and because gamblers hope they will double in price. This condition always has prevailed in the third phase of bull markets."

The bull market which began in 1942 hit its peak in May, 1946, with the D-J Industrials at 212.50 (see

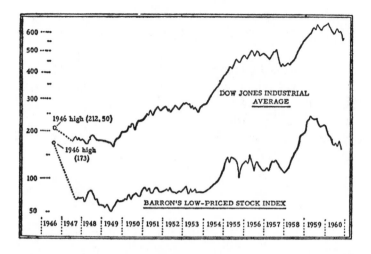

chart). Barron's Low-Priced Stock Index (a convenient measure of low-priced stock activity) recorded its third phase high of 173 in February, 1946, two months earlier. Traditionally, the low-priced stocks establish their bull market highs before the final "topping out" of the high-grade D-J Industrials. The reason for this is that the low-priced stocks (which lack professional or institutional sponsorship) are usually "dumped" or "unloaded" after a sharp advance, whereas the high grade stocks are systematically distributed.

From a 1946 high of 173, Barron's L-P Stock Index declined to a low of 50.74 on June 30, 1949. From there the Index moved upwards again, rising gradually through the period of the early 1950's. By 1953 Barron's L-P Stock Index touched 90, having barely kept pace (in percentages) with the advance of the D-J Industrials. During the broad second phase advance of 1953–56 the D-J Industrial Average doubled, climbing from 255 to 521. During the same period Barron's L-P Stock Index advanced from 75 to a 1956 peak of 150. Again the L-P Index managed only to keep up with the movements of the high-grade Industrials. It is interesting to note that by 1956 the D-J Industrials had climbed almost 150% above their peak price of 1946, yet the supposedly volatile L-P Index had not even approached the old 1946 high of 173. In other words, nothing in the action of the L-P Stock Index during the years from 1949 to 1956 suggested that the market had seen a typical third phase "boom."

During the reaction of 1957 the L-P Index sank somewhat lower, but it held well above its low of 1955. Despite the opinion (widely held in 1957) that a "bear market" was in progress, the action of the L-P Stock Index implied nothing of the sort. Prior to July, 1957 low-priced stocks had *not engaged in major upward moves* as they had in 1928–29, 1936–37 and 1945–46. By the same token, during the reaction of 1957 low-priced stocks had *not collapsed* as had been the case following 1929, 1937 and 1946.

The period of 1958 and early 1959 saw the low-priced stocks make their first great bull market advances. Between December, 1957, and April, 1958, Barron's L-P Stock Index doubled. The Index hit a high of 250 in April, 1959, a full three months before the bull market "topped out." Since April, 1959, the L-P Index has dropped steadily, touching a low of 163.7 in the last week of October, 1960. This means that low-priced stocks, as measured by Barron's Index, have lost 34% of their value in the first year-and-a-half of the bear market. As is their habit during the earlier stages of a bear market, the low-priced stocks declined about twice as fast as the high-grade D-J Industrial stocks.

To sum up, the violent movement of low-priced stocks, both on the advance of 1958–59 and on the decline of 1959–60, was in marked contrast to the generally sluggish action of this group before and after the 1957 reaction. Furthermore, since the last quarter of 1958 the average yield on the D-J Industrials has remained in the dangerous 3½% area, a phenomenon which has not been seen since 1946. In view of the timing element, the volatile movements of the low-priced stocks and the contrasting yield factor, there is ample evidence to suggest that the current market is fundamentally different from the one which existed in 1957.

❧ ❧